RESEARCH APPROACHES TO SUPPORTING STUDENTS ON THE AUTISM SPECTRUM IN INCLUSIVE SCHOOLS

This book will support researchers in the field of education disability by outlining inclusive research approaches and their challenges, outcomes, and impact. Each chapter reports on school/university-based research supporting inclusion for young people on the autism spectrum. This research has been developed in Australian schools with students, families, teachers, and specialists. The intent of this approach is to mobilise new knowledge to the benefit of all students, including students on the autism spectrum, their families, teachers, and school communities. This book showcases how research can be more inclusive with a move to collaborative, participatory, and co-produced research that will impact on young people, families, and educators. The authors highlight the complex challenges and the positive outcomes of conducting research in inclusive ways and provide detailed practical strategies for researchers.

Inclusive education is socially, emotionally, and academically beneficial for all students and positively impacts on respectful attitudes to difference. This book provides a groundbreaking approach to research that by design is inclusive and therefore provides an invaluable opportunity for building the foundations of an inclusive society for all. This book will be invaluable to researchers, educators, and professional learning in schools.

Suzanne Carrington is a Professor in education at QUT Australia. She has over 25 years of experience working in universities in teaching, research, international development, and senior leadership roles. Suzanne's areas of expertise are in inclusive education, ethical leadership, and disability impacting on policy and practice in Australian and international contexts.

Beth Saggers is an Associate Professor in the School of Early Childhood and Inclusive Education at QUT Australia.

Keely Harper-Hill is the Research Associate for the Enhancing Learning and Teaching education research program of the Autism CRC at QUT Australia.

Michael Whelan is an Associate Professor in the School of Creative Practice at QUT Australia. He is also a writer, musician, and autism advocate.

COVER ART

Layers of Community
Our autistic community is our strength through the layers of support that we share in our peers, families, and professionals. No two autistic people are the same shape or colour but with the right layers of support we celebrate neurodiversity.

Artist's name – Leeann Friday

RESEARCH APPROACHES TO SUPPORTING STUDENTS ON THE AUTISM SPECTRUM IN INCLUSIVE SCHOOLS

Outcomes, Challenges, and Impact

*Suzanne Carrington, Beth Saggers,
Keely Harper-Hill, and Michael Whelan*

LONDON AND NEW YORK

First published 2021
by Routledge
2 Park Square, Milton Park, Abingdon, Oxon OX14 4RN

and by Routledge
52 Vanderbilt Avenue, New York, NY 10017

Routledge is an imprint of the Taylor & Francis Group, an informa business

© 2021 Autism CRC

The right of Suzanne Carrington, Beth Saggers, Keely Harper-Hill, and Michael Whelan to be identified as the authors of this work has been asserted in accordance with sections 77 and 78 of the Copyright, Designs and Patents Act 1988.

All rights reserved. No part of this book may be reprinted or reproduced or utilised in any form or by any electronic, mechanical, or other means, now known or hereafter invented, including photocopying and recording, or in any information storage or retrieval system, without permission in writing from the publishers.

Trademark notice: Product or corporate names may be trademarks or registered trademarks and are used only for identification and explanation without intent to infringe.

British Library Cataloguing-in-Publication Data
A catalogue record for this book is available from the British Library

Library of Congress Cataloging-in-Publication Data
A catalog record has been requested for this book

ISBN: 978-0-367-50184-6 (hbk)
ISBN: 978-0-367-50187-7 (pbk)
ISBN: 978-1-003-04908-1 (ebk)

Typeset in Bembo
by SPi Global, India

We dedicate this book to Emeritus Professor Sylvia Rodger AM. Sylvia's leadership in the development of the Autism CRC ensured that our School Years Program research is inclusive, multidisciplinary, and high-quality. Sylvia was passionate about meeting the needs of young people, their families, and educators in order that students are successful at school and beyond. We believe that she would be proud of our collective work.

Emeritus Professor Sylvia Rodger AM

CONTENTS

Figures and tables ix
Foreword x
Acknowledgements xiii
Contributors xv

PART 1
Introduction 1

1 An introduction to research in inclusive education: Empirical evidence for supporting an inclusive approach for students on the autism spectrum 3
   Suzanne Carrington and Beth Saggers

2 Inclusive research practice: Engaging autistic individuals and their families in research 17
   Wenn B. Lawson and Suzanne Carrington

PART 2
Outcomes of an inclusive research approach 33

3 Supporting students on the autism spectrum in inclusive schools: Research to inform implementation of support and evidence-based practices 35
   Beth Saggers and Suzanne Carrington

4 Autistic voices in autism education research 50
   Trudy Bartlett and Suzanne Carrington

PART 3
Knowledge translation and research impact 67

5 With teachers, for teachers: Knowledge translation and professional learning 69
   Michael Whelan, Jeremy Kerr, Keely Harper-Hill, and Oksana Zelenko

6 Meeting the needs of all: The case to translate the evidence base beyond autism 88
   Keely Harper-Hill, Michael Whelan, and Beth Saggers

7 Developing communities of practice for educator professional learning – Developing connections in rural and remote regions 102
   Chris Edwards and Beth Saggers

PART 4
Conclusion 119

8 Summary and propositions 121
   Keely Harper-Hill, Suzanne Carrington, Beth Saggers, and Michael Whelan

Index *130*

FIGURES AND TABLES

Figures

4.1	Hyposensitivity and the autistic brain	56
4.2	Hypersensitivity and the autistic brain	57
5.1	Co-design workshop: Three online and two in-person	74
5.2	Design researcher Dr Jeremy Kerr facilitates an online co-design session: Five online and two in-person	75
5.3	Stages in visual and thematic analysis	77
5.4	Prototype homepage: Provisional title: *Diverse Learners Hub*	79
5.5	Prototype: Practice categories	80
5.6	Real-time onscreen display of teacher response to a question. Brisbane Catholic Education (Springwood)	81
5.7	*inclusionED* – Teacher practice	84
5.8	*inclusionED* – Implementation	85
7.1	Communities of practice: Conceptual diagram	103

Table

7.1	*Summary of the Tele-Classroom Consultation Approach*	107

FOREWORD

I am delighted to introduce this publication, *'Research approaches to supporting students on the autism spectrum in inclusive schools: Outcomes, challenges, and impact'*.

This is one of two volumes written to support researchers, teachers, and specialists working to develop inclusive educational environments and programs for students on the autism spectrum.

This, the *Research* volume, supports researchers seeking to support neurodiverse students in education, including those on the autism spectrum. It provides the reader with an understanding of the challenges inherent in translating research into classroom practice, providing recommendations for future approaches and a framework for inclusive research in education. Its companion volume, *'Supporting students on the autism spectrum in inclusive schools: A practical guide to implementing evidence-based approaches'*, provides practice guidance and resources for educators and school communities to support students and their learning.

Autism is a collective term for a group of neurodevelopmental conditions that affect social interaction, communication, behaviours, and interests. Every person on the autism spectrum is unique, having their own strengths and challenges. The developmental challenges and their presentation can vary widely in nature and severity between individuals, and in the same individual over time. Many people on the spectrum experience additional challenges with educational and vocational attainment, important pillars for social and economic participation, health, and well-being. The latest Australian data show that only 26% of autistic adolescents are likely to go on to complete post-secondary education and training, significantly less than for all people with disability (45.5%) and for those without a disability (59.3%).

In 2013, Autism CRC established the world's first national, cooperative research effort focused on autism across the lifespan – through a formal venture between the research, service, government, and autism community sectors – and supported by the Australian Government's Cooperative Research Centre Program. Our national program of research and its translation to practice and policy spanned the early childhood years, the school years, and adulthood.

Autism CRC's School Years Program is built on our foundational research undertaken in Australia's first nationwide needs analysis of the educational needs of autistic students (aged 5–16 years). This study identified the priorities for research based on inputs from almost 1,500 school administrators, teachers and specialist support staff, ancillary support staff such as teacher aides, parents, and students.

Autism CRC's work is underpinned by a commitment to inclusive research practices and co-production with those on the spectrum, their families, and those who strive to support them, and this is evident in the research that underpins this volume. Over the past six years, the School Years Program has directly involved more than 3,000 educators, 7,000 students, and 1,300 parents and carers along with allied health workers, psychologists, and support people in research program design, development, and evaluation. It has seen more than 25 research projects conducted on-ground in 300+ state, Catholic and independent schools across Australia, which have developed:

- tools and practices to enhance teaching and the learning experience (classrooms of excellence);
- evidence-based tools and programs for supporting social, emotional, and behavioural needs of children and adolescents;
- a better understanding of the developmental and behavioural trajectories of students on the autism spectrum; and
- the skills and confidence of teachers and support personnel.

Overseeing this vast array of projects and diverse cast of researchers, organisations, education departments, teachers, parents, carers, and students has been Suzanne Carrington, School Years Program Director at Autism CRC and Professor in the Faculty of Education at the Queensland University of Technology. Suzanne and her team of researchers are dedicated to the principles of inclusive education and Universal Design for Learning as an effective framework for providing support for the needs of all students in inclusive schools, including those on the autism spectrum.

A 2018 Australian Bureau of Statistics study found that 31.2% of students with disabilities are placed in special classes in mainstream schools or special schools, while the figure is 40.8% for students on the autism spectrum. The data also reveal that 77.7% of autistic individuals attending school or another educational institution reported social, learning, and communication difficulties at their place of learning. These findings reflect that greater identification and presence of students on the spectrum in mainstream education have not been accompanied by adequate educational supports in response to their needs.

At the same time, evidence indicates that inclusive education benefits all students, those with and without disability. Herein lies our challenge.

I hope that the learnings contained in this volume will influence positive change in our education systems and schools as we strive for truly inclusive and equitable education for all.

As you read through this book, and its companion *Practice* volume, I hope you enjoy the beautiful artwork. In 2014, 2016, and 2018, Autism CRC held an Art Prize inviting people on the autism spectrum to showcase their strengths and interests through art. The response was excellent and some of the wonderful examples are displayed on the cover and throughout the volumes.

I express my sincere thanks to many thousands of students, parents, education, and allied health professionals that have contributed to the outcomes of our School Years Program. My thanks also to the many research team members and the authors of this book for their tireless commitment to our work. I know they join me in dedicating this volume to Emeritus Professor Sylvia Rodger AM, Autism CRC's founder, whose vision and passion continue to inspire us.

I hope you find *Research approaches to supporting students on the autism spectrum in inclusive schools: Outcomes, challenges, and impact* insightful as we work towards building a more inclusive education environment for all learners.

Andrew Davis
Chief Executive Officer
Autism CRC

ACKNOWLEDGEMENTS

We would like to acknowledge and thank the researchers, our co-authors who have worked with us on the chapters in this book. Our co-authors share our vision for improving the lives of young people on the autism spectrum and supporting inclusive education. Thank you for the collaboration and ongoing professional conversations. We look forward to our future work together.

We would like to acknowledge all of our education partners, schools, the autistic community, students, and parents as this research could not have happened without your great and unwavering support. It has been our privilege to work with you over the past seven years. We hope this book supports our ongoing shared passion and commitment to inclusion.

We would also like to acknowledge Julie Nickerson for her enormous and magnificent contribution to this book. Julie supported our work as authors, co-authors, managed all of the communication with our publisher, managed the internal review processes, the permissions for artwork, communications with the Autism CRC, and was amazing and good fun to work with! Thank you, Julie!!

Finally, we would like to thank Andrew Davis, the Chief Executive Officer, Autism CRC, Therese Conway, the Research Program Manager, Autism CRC, and the review team that she coordinated. Our collective work has been improved after receiving your thoughtful comments and feedback. Thank you!

The artwork featured in this book from 'The Autism CRC Art Prize' (2016) and 'The Autism CRC Digital Art Celebration' (2018) has been provided with permission by:

Leeann Friday: *Layers of Community* (Front cover)
Sarah Harding: *My Helping Hands* (Part 1 title page)
Toby Prendergast: *Birds of Differences* (Part 2 title page)

Imogen: *Cogs Will Turn Just Differently* (Part 3 title page)
Amy Forbes-Richardson: *The Gamut* (Part 4 title page)
The authors kindly thank these artists for the use of their work which has brought the pages to life.

CONTRIBUTORS

Trudy Bartlett is a High School Special Education Teacher currently at Marsden State High School, Queensland, Australia. Her areas of expertise are in inclusive education, teaching students on the autism spectrum and reasonable adjustments to curriculum and assessment. She is a proud autistic educator and regularly consults for Autism Spectrum Australia (ASPECT) and Autism CRC. She is currently a classroom special education teacher, a case manager of students with disabilities and leads a Professional Learning Community titled *Removing learner barriers for autistic students*. She has been a Football Queensland Futsal (FQF) representative player since 2011. She has been the FQF Athletes with Disabilities Futsal state coach since 2015. In her time as a Queensland representative player and coach, she has won multiple National Titles, and in 2019, she was appointed the Australian Athletes with Disabilities Futsal Goal Keeper Coach where she travelled with the Australian team to the INAS Global Games for athletes with intellectual disabilities.

Suzanne Carrington is a Professor at the Queensland University of Technology, Australia. Her areas of expertise are in inclusive education, disability, and teacher preparation for inclusive schools. She has engaged in research to inform policy and practice in Australian and international education contexts, more recently extending this research to the South Pacific and Asia. She has broad knowledge of education research, and her publication list provides evidence of extensive collaboration with education and health research. Currently she is the Program Director of the School Years Program for the Cooperative Research Centre for Living with Autism (Autism CRC). This is the world's first cooperative research centre focused on autism across the lifespan.

Chris Edwards completed his PhD as part of the Cooperative Research Centre for Living with Autism (Autism CRC). This research was conducted through the

School of Early Childhood and Inclusive Education at Queensland University of Technology. His doctoral research explored an innovative approach to service delivery, utilising teleconsultation to support communities of practice for educators of young learners on the autism spectrum in rural and remote regions. In addition to his research experience, Chris has a background in behavioural science (psychology) and over five years of experience supporting a diverse range of learning needs in children and adults.

Keely Harper-Hill, PhD, is the Research Associate in the education program of research of the Cooperative Research Centre for Living with Autism (Autism CRC) and is based in the Office of Education Research at the Queensland University of Technology. Keely's interest in supporting the educational needs of students on the autism spectrum began in the early 1990s from her clinical work as a speech pathologist in school settings. Her research interests include language processing, educational listening environments, and how students on the autism spectrum are supported to participate in the classroom and access the curriculum.

Jeremy Kerr is a senior lecturer for the Visual Communication Program, and a design practitioner with over 20 years industry experience. Jeremy's research focus lies in the exploration and development of design and design frameworks to advance community capacity building and self-advocacy. His current research includes design-led initiatives in the areas of mental health and wellbeing, intercultural design, children's health and nutrition, and in the disability sector. A core aspect of his work is applying co-design methodologies to foster collaboration and to include the authentic voice and creative input of stakeholders in design solutions.

Wenn B. Lawson (PhD), an autistic lecturer, psychologist, researcher, advocate, writer, and poet, has passionately shared his professional and personal knowledge regarding autism for 25 years. He has written and/or contributed to over 25 books and many papers. Wenn is a teaching Fellow with the University of Birmingham's Masters Autism course (UK), a senior researcher with Macquarie University and Curtin University, Australia, a participant with the Cooperative Research Centre for Living with Autism (Autism CRC), Co-Chair of the Autism Research Council Australia, ambassador for the 'I CAN' agency of Australia, and resides on the Editorial Board for the journal, *Autism in Adulthood*. Wenn is a family man with autistic adult offspring and autistic grandchildren. In 2017 he presented to the United Nations on matters of autism and ageing.

Beth Saggers is an Associate Professor in the School of Early Childhood and Inclusive Education at Queensland University of Technology, Australia. She currently lectures in autism spectrum, catering for diversity, inclusive practices, and supporting challenging and complex needs, mental health and wellbeing, and social emotional support. She has over 30 years of experience working with students on the autism spectrum across a range of age groups and educational settings. She is an active research participant in the Cooperative Research Centre for Living with Autism (Autism CRC). Her research interests include developing supportive learning environments for students on the autism spectrum, the perspectives of key stakeholders, collaborative partnerships, and supporting challenging and complex student needs.

Michael Whelan is an Associate Professor in the School of Creative Practice in the Creative Industries Faculty at Queensland University of Technology in Australia. In addition to his memoir, *The Other Country: A Father's Journey with Autism* which was published by Pan Macmillan in 2008, Michael also wrote the documentary film *What are you doing?* This educational film for school audiences on the topic of social inclusion and autism was distributed to every school in Australia and was screened at the United Nations in New York as part of World Autism Day activities in April, 2013. Michael's current research is focused upon knowledge translation of autism research for application by mainstream teachers of students with diverse learning needs.

Oksana Zelenko holds the role of Director, Research Engagement and Impact, with Creative Industries Faculty, Queensland University of Technology (QUT). Previously she was Discipline Leader heading up several design departments, including Industrial Design, Interaction Design, Visual Communication and Fashion at QUT School of Design. Her area of expertise is in design research for eHealth applications with a specific focus on using participatory and co-design methods for digital health, specifically in the area of youth mental health and wellbeing. Oksana has led and contributed to a range of national and international research projects resulting in innovative digital health applications, including award-winning mHealth apps. She regularly presents her research nationally and internationally and is the co-editor of *Design and Ethics: Reflections on Practice* published by Routledge.

PART 1
Introduction

My Helping Hands (by Sarah Harding, aged nine years)

'This shows how I think a lot about my friends and how I can help them and others.'

1

AN INTRODUCTION TO RESEARCH IN INCLUSIVE EDUCATION

Empirical evidence for supporting an inclusive approach for students on the autism spectrum

Suzanne Carrington and Beth Saggers

This chapter sets the agenda for this book by introducing the research supporting inclusive education. Inclusive education leads to positive academic and social emotional outcomes for all students, with and without disabilities. An inclusive approach was a focus of the research in the Cooperative Research Centre for Living with Autism (Autism CRC) and our researchers worked with educators, families, and students in classrooms and schools to establish evidence to inform inclusive practice. The research reported in this chapter is an important starting point for this book and will influence how education systems, schools, and teachers commit to inclusive education in the future. This chapter defines inclusive education and describes the difference between inclusive education and special education. We suggest that it is important to understand the difference before we consider how we can support advocacy and promote change in policy and practice. The chapter presents research to support short-term and long-term benefits of an inclusive approach. Further to this discussion, the chapter will specifically present an overview of the evidence drawn from international research that focuses on inclusive education for students on the autism spectrum. This chapter provides evidence to support future policy and planning for improved inclusive education programs and builds a shared understanding that inclusive education is a global movement to support equitable and quality education. The research reported in this book highlights how the social and cultural context of education communities is important and that educators, families, and students need to work together in respectful ways to support inclusion and a sense of belonging for all.

Inclusive education is now viewed as a human right where all students, whether they have a disability or not, have the right to access, be successful, and participate at their local school (United Nations, 2006). The UN *Convention on the Rights of Persons with Disabilities* (CRPD) was published in 2006 and ratified by more than 180 countries, making inclusive education a legally binding obligation for countries such as Australia under Article 24. This is reinforced through the companion document, *General Comment 4*, released in 2016, which now provides a clear definition of inclusion:

> Inclusion involves a process of systemic reform embodying changes and modifications in content, teaching methods, approaches, structures and strategies in education to overcome barriers with a vision serving to provide all students of the relevant age range with an equitable and participatory learning experience and environment that best corresponds to their requirements and preferences.
>
> (United Nations, 2016, p. 4)

Inclusive education is also a goal in the *2030 Agenda for Sustainable Development* and the *Sustainable Development Goals* (SDGs).[1] The signing of international declarations such as the CRPD by countries around the world means that inclusive education at local mainstream schools is the expected approach for students with disabilities and that special education should be phased out over time (UNESCO, 2017; United Nations, 2006). The research reported in this book aims to support educators to include autistic students in their local schools, transition to life after school, and to participate meaningfully in their community. The authors share their research approaches and outcomes of working in respectful and inclusive ways to support the development of culture, policy, and practice for inclusion.

> ...all students, whether they have a disability or not, have the right to access, be successful, and participate at their local school

What is the difference between inclusive education and special education?

It is important to understand the difference between inclusive education and special education before we consider how we can support advocacy and promote change in policy and practice. Special education is often considered as an approach to inclusive education in countries such as Australia where there is an array of special education options currently in place. These include: special and segregated schools; special satellite classes that are situated in the grounds of mainstream schools; special supports and programs that aim to operate in more inclusive ways in mainstream schools; and mainstream schools that have embedded tiers of support for all students in inclusive mainstream classrooms. However, segregated and special models of support cannot be described as inclusive education programs.

We believe that in order to move forward to a more inclusive approach, it is necessary to discuss the historical changes that have informed how students with disability are viewed and supported in education. For decades, the medical model of disability has dominated the identification and educational support of students with disabilities worldwide. The key assumption in this model is that students with a disability represent a deviation from the norm and have a deficit or disorder that requires treatment to fit into society and into schools (Carrington & MacArthur, 2012). More recently, professional and autistic people prefer to view autism as a different way of seeing the world and suggest that the terms 'disorder' and 'disability' are more reflective of a medical condition, suggesting that autism is something that can be cured (Kenny et al., 2016). Supporting students with a disability in special schools or classrooms has been a long-standing paradigm in education, underpinned by the beliefs and assumptions of the medical model of disability (Hansen, Carrington, Jensen, Molbæk, & Schmidt, 2020). The separation of students with a disability into segregated and special places is influenced by the social and cultural expectations in a particular context and the judgements about difference. Special placement in segregated settings for children with disabilities has resulted in a marginalised population that has been institutionalised, undereducated, socially rejected, and excluded from society (Biklen, 1988). These types of outcomes are not the result of the disability but are the result of the social, economic, and political actions such as special education. The beliefs and assumptions may be submerged in the routine of work and thoughts of educators and perpetuated by systems of schooling (Carrington, 1999).

> *It is important to understand the difference between inclusive education and special education*

In contrast, the social model of disability (Oliver, 1996) promoted in this book places emphasis on the social context and the impact of society on individuals. This perspective considers the ways that the environment (physical and social) is constructed and responds to individuals with an impairment. This model represents a shift in our thinking and understanding of difference, as it asks us to reconsider how our societal norms, beliefs, values, and behaviours can create a disability or a problem within individuals. The social model view has guided the development of inclusive school communities, where difference is regarded as a natural part of human diversity and is respected and celebrated. As stated by Carrington, Mann, and Mavropoulou (2019, p. 4):

> A critical implication of this model is that all students, irrespective of their level of (dis)ability, belong and will be educated in the same inclusive educational context and it is the responsibility of educators to ensure that all students will have access to the same learning opportunities by removing any barriers encountered by students with disabilities.

Therefore, inclusive education requires teachers and other educators to challenge their understanding of difference in order to have an explicit values base that draws on a social-cultural perspective of diversity in society. This is a different paradigm to the medical and deficit model that informs special education. In an inclusive education model, disability can be viewed as just one form of socially constructed difference and different societies react to many kinds of difference. It is the cultural and social constructions of difference and school success and failure that are represented in beliefs, attitudes, and values and shape how teachers and educators interact with students (Carrington, 1999).

In the research presented in this book, we want to encourage cooperation between special schools and mainstream schools as this provides opportunities to share specialist knowledge and skills that are necessary to support students with disabilities such as autism. The expected cooperation will also inform open discussion that would support transition to more inclusive approaches to education (Ainscow, 2007). The key message is that governments need to make a clear commitment to inclusion and emphasise the benefits for parents, children, and the broader community. This requires a transformation of education systems, and teacher knowledge and skills. de Bruin (2019) reported that students on the autism spectrum continue to be segregated and indicates that the legislative reforms associated with the CRPD are not enough. She highlights the lack of transparency of placement and enrolment data for students with disabilities, such as autism, and suggests that there is an urgent necessity to support student placement in regular classes.

Translating inclusive education policy to practice

It is now widely acknowledged that inclusive education leads to positive academic and social emotional outcomes for all students, with and without disabilities (Cole, Murphy, Frisby, Grossi, & Bolte, 2019; Cologon, 2013, 2019; Hehir et al., 2016; Ruijs & Peetsma, 2009; Szumski, Smogorzewska, & Karwowski, 2017). However, while it has been clearly established that the outcomes are positive for everyone involved (Cologon, 2019), there are still many challenges of translating inclusive education policy to school reform and practice. Considering this challenge, we acknowledge that context is important in shaping inclusive education policies and strategic plans. When we consider context, we need to acknowledge geography, history (colonisation, aid, domestic, etc.), policies (local, national, regional, international), culture, and religion (Beutel, Tangen, & Carrington, 2019; Harris & Jones, 2018; Kozleski, Artiles, & Waitoller, 2014). Recent work in developing inclusive education policy and initiatives in international contexts (Carrington et al., 2019; Duke et al., 2016) highlights the need to respect the social and cultural values of countries that are receiving support. In many countries, there is evidence that religious beliefs and attitudes influence how people conceptualise understanding of disability as karma or fate and this influences suppression of people with disabilities in communities (Miles, 2013). A recent study by Subba et al. (2019) has documented that teachers and principals hold beliefs in karmic actions that support the segregation of persons with disability. An understanding of culture

> ...inclusive education leads to positive academic and social emotional outcomes for all students, with and without disabilities

and context informs our focus on working with education systems, governments, school leaders, teachers, parents, and students in the context of schools to conduct collaborative research that will optimise students' social, behavioural, and academic success at school and beyond. A further consideration is about the positive attitudes and the impact of confidence that teachers have in their knowledge and skills in teaching within inclusive settings.

It is generally understood that education staff need to be confident, have a positive attitude, and have the knowledge and skills to teach all students using an inclusive approach (Cologon, 2019). The research approach and outcomes reported in the following chapters highlight the respect that our researchers have for teachers and specialists working to support students on the spectrum in education settings. We understand that working in inclusive ways requires new thinking and practice and we have a collective focus on knowledge translation from our research to ensure impact on practice in schools. This will be discussed in more detail in Part 3 of this book (Chapters 5, 6, and 7). We have evidence that shows participation in our research projects supports inclusion and has influenced professional growth and increased personal satisfaction (Saggers, Tones, Dunne, & Aberdein, 2019). Research has also indicated that when teachers develop skills to support inclusion of students with disabilities, this also results in higher-quality teaching for all students and more confident teachers (Hehir & Katzman, 2012; Jordan, Glenn, & McGhie-Richmond, 2010). The evidence base which supports and influences our knowledge, understanding, and implementation of inclusive research approaches for students on the autism spectrum will now be presented.

> ...working in inclusive ways requires new thinking and practice

Evidence to support inclusive education for students on the autism spectrum

To date, evidence supporting inclusive education for students on the autism spectrum through measurement of educational outcomes has been mixed (Humphrey & Symes, 2013; Jordan, 2008; Locke, Shih, Kretzmann, & Kasari, 2016; Reed & Osborne, 2014; Roberts & Simpson, 2016). While some studies have highlighted positive outcomes of inclusion for students on the autism spectrum (Sansosti & Sansosti, 2012), others have found few differences between segregated and inclusive settings (Osborne & Reed, 2011; Waddington & Reed, 2006) and no uniformity or consistency in positive outcomes reported (Sansosti & Sansosti, 2012). In most instances, it is not so much that outcomes are not evident but rather that currently there is a paucity of evidence well-articulated in research particularly in relation to academic and social outcomes with studies limited in scope and sample size (Ferraioli & Harris, 2011).

Despite the current shortfalls in research into inclusive education for students on the spectrum, a recent review of research investigating different stakeholders' perspectives (educators, parents, and students on the spectrum) of inclusive education for students on the spectrum highlighted some key beneficial outcomes (Roberts & Simpson, 2016). These outcomes included: i) promoting awareness and acceptance of diversity; ii) reducing stigma; and iii) providing an opportunity for students on the spectrum and their peers to experience new social situations and develop social skills alongside one another (Roberts & Simpson, 2016). Previous research investigating outcomes in inclusive settings has found the following positive outcomes for students with disabilities including students on the spectrum:

- Higher levels of engagement and social interaction.
- Students give and receive higher levels of social support.
- Wider social networks.
- More advanced individual education goals than their counterparts in segregated settings.
- Increased opportunities to engage with more positive role models.
(Eldar, Talmor, & Wolf-Zukerman, 2010)

The findings of this research by Eldar et al. (2010) identified two major factors impacting upon the success of inclusive settings for students on the spectrum. These factors were as follows: i) internal factors linked to the student's social, behavioural, and cognitive level that impacted on the type of strategies and adjustments to the environment that were required; and ii) external factors linked to the inclusive environment including collaboration, attitudes, and organisational aspects of the environment.

External factors can facilitate inclusive learning environments for all students. Extending the findings of Eldar et al. (2010), a more recent review of research investigating stakeholders' perspectives of inclusion of students on the autism spectrum (Roberts & Simpson, 2016) identified three key external factors that promoted inclusion in schools. These factors included: i) attitudes towards inclusion; ii) knowledge and understanding of autism; and iii) type of support. These three factors that influence the success of inclusion for students on the spectrum will now be discussed in more detail.

External factor 1: Attitudes towards inclusion

Research evidence promotes the importance of positive attitudes towards inclusion as influencing students' success in inclusive settings (Cologon, 2019). Waddington and Reed (2006) highlighted the importance that parents and educators place on a school settings' commitment and willingness to accept students on the autism spectrum as a key factor in influencing positive outcomes. In addition, other research (e.g., Humphrey & Symes, 2013; Roberts & Simpson, 2016; Segall & Campbell, 2012; Whitaker, 2007) highlights that school communities, education professionals, and parents generally hold a positive attitude towards inclusive education for students on the spectrum and that this positively influences the success of inclusion and the implementation of inclusive practices within school communities.

External factor 2: Knowledge and understanding of autism

Other research has identified educators' professional knowledge and understanding of the autism spectrum as critical to successful inclusion for students on the spectrum. This factor has been identified by educators, parents, and professionals as essential to the success of inclusion for this group of students (Iadarola et al., 2015; Jackson Brewin, Renwick, & Schormans, 2008; Mayton, 2004; Saggers, Tones, Dunne, Trembath, et al., 2019; Sansosti & Sansosti, 2012; Segall & Campbell, 2012; Yumak & Akgul, 2010) and in helping educators identify and implement effective strategies to support the learning of students on the spectrum in inclusive settings.

External factor 3: Type of support

The importance of appropriate support is a significant factor supporting positive outcomes for students on the autism spectrum in inclusive settings. This support includes structural support within education settings in the form of resources, funding, and appropriate personnel to support inclusive outcomes. Home–school communication has also been identified as important in supporting positive inclusive outcomes. A lack of resources, funding, limited access to multidisciplinary support, and a lack of time to consult and collaborate with parents, colleagues, and multidisciplinary teams are considered barriers to successful inclusive outcomes (Saggers et al., 2018). Further challenges faced by students on the autism spectrum in inclusive settings will now be considered in more detail.

Challenges of inclusive approaches

Despite a focus on inclusive education for all students, many students on the autism spectrum continue to experience challenges related to: accessing, participating in, and engaging in inclusive education programs; achieving successful educational outcomes; and receiving appropriate support (Humphrey & Symes, 2013; Lindsay, Ricketts, Peacey, Dockrell, & Charman, 2016). Additionally, school communities often experience challenges identifying and implementing appropriate practices to effectively meet the needs of this group of students and allowing them to maximise their educational potential. Research evidence has identified that students on the autism spectrum underperform relative to their level of ability and experience difficulties maintaining their attention and regulating their emotions and behaviours in inclusive settings even with specialised support in place (Ashburner, Ziviani, & Rodger, 2010). In addition, they experience poorer educational and post-school outcomes than other students (Estes, Rivera, Bryan, Cali, & Dawson, 2011; Jones et al., 2009; Keen, Webster, & Ridley, 2015). According to the most recent Australian Institute of Health and Welfare (AIHW) survey results released by the Australian Bureau of Statistics (AIHW, 2017), some of the most challenging aspects of schooling include:

- Fitting in socially.
- Learning difficulties.
- Communication difficulties.

In addition, research indicates that students on the spectrum are at a higher risk of being bullied, especially if they are in mainstream settings (Saggers et al., 2017). This is despite the fact that it is now estimated that 73% of students are educated in a mainstream setting (AIHW, 2017). These findings highlight the need to identify challenges and make adjustments to the context that address the needs of this group of students to enable success.

The social communication needs and challenging behaviours often experienced by students on the autism spectrum have been identified as having an impact on inclusion, with relationships between educators and students as well as between affected students (Saggers, Hwang, & Mercer, 2011). In the recent *Australian Autism Educational Needs Analysis* project (Saggers et al., 2018), when asking students on the spectrum to identify key challenges at school, several key factors were highlighted as most challenging to deal with:

- Social demands.
- The need for proficient use of executive function skills to manage the organisation and planning aspects of the school environment.
- Coping with the handwriting demands.
- Coping with the transition and change that occurs on a regular basis in the school environment.
- Regulating their emotions (e.g., managing anxiety and staying calm).

In addition, students identified that the three sensory elements of the school environment that had the most impact and were most challenging to manage were noise, touch, and having to stay still.

The same study highlighted from a parent, educator, and specialist perspective that it was the social emotional needs followed by the behavioural and communication needs of students on the autism spectrum that were most challenging to effectively support in the school environment (Saggers et al., 2018). A key challenge in schools remains a lack of necessary support at all levels: individual; class; and whole of school (Roberts & Simpson, 2016). This has been identified as a key reason for a school placement to fail (Roberts & Simpson, 2016) and has implications for work moving forward with successful outcomes in the inclusion space.

> A key challenge in schools remains a lack of necessary support at all levels: individual; class; and whole of school

Support that has been highlighted as necessary to support the challenges identified include reduced class sizes; more teacher time for collaboration; availability of support personnel; and access to multidisciplinary support (Roberts & Simpson, 2016; Saggers et al., 2018). Environmental supports that allow for quiet or sanctuary spaces and reduce the sensory feedback from the environment (e.g., noise), as well as personnel to support transition, individual social, academic, and behavioural needs when necessary, along with academic and assessment adjustments as required, have also been identified (Roberts & Simpson, 2016; Saggers et al., 2018). More education and training in inclusive practices and the autism spectrum to build knowledge and understanding have also been identified as necessary moving forward (Roberts & Simpson, 2016; Saggers et al., 2018). Leadership and policy which will provide support and guidance to schools as they transition to a more inclusive approach will be needed to ensure the success of these requirements, and this will now be discussed in the following section.

Future policy and planning in Australia

Because Australia is one of the signatory countries to the CRPD (United Nations, 2006), we have a legally binding obligation to provide inclusive education in our schools. Over the years, Australian parliaments have enacted anti-discrimination legislation that include the *Disability Standards for Education 2005* (reviewed in 2015) (Australian Government, 2005) under the *Disability Discrimination Act 1992* (Australian Government, 2018). The Department of Education, Queensland, which is a state in Australia, states, 'Inclusion is embedded in all aspects of school life, and is supported by culture, polices and every day practices' (Queensland Government, 2018). This type of statement necessitates an ethical approach to leadership in schools (Carrington & Kimber, 2020). Ethical leaders need to work with members of their school community, and model inclusive and ethical practice (Ehrich & Carrington, 2018) by documenting and communicating a clear vision and shared set of values for working towards inclusion (Cologon, 2019).

Research to date has emphasised the importance of building school capacity and nurturing a whole-school approach to inclusion that supports the needs of all students including those on the autism spectrum. Critical to this is building school capacity to support the needs of students on the autism spectrum through: knowledge translation and awareness; funding; appropriate environmental adjustments and supports; and the nurturing of collaborative partnerships (Saggers, Tones, Dunne, Trembath, et al., 2019).

Considering that inclusive education at local mainstream schools is the expected approach for students with disabilities and that special education should be phased out over time (UNESCO, 2017; United Nations, 2016), we need to consider what is needed to support changes in policy and planning in the future. One important area of consideration is teacher education.

Teacher education for inclusive education

Teacher education has been criticised as being inadequate to support teachers for teaching in inclusive schools (Hemmings & Woodcock, 2011) and is a major international area of concern. It is clear that pre-service and in-service teacher education programs can have a positive impact on attitudes and confidence, and support the development of skills and knowledge to support an inclusive approach. Cologon (2019) summarises the research and presents the key elements of teacher education that result in more positive attitudes and understanding of inclusive education. Some key elements include:

- A human rights-based approach to inclusive education for all students.
- Critical reflection and consciousness to support positive attitudes.

- Support in developing skills for addressing barriers to inclusive education.
- Consideration of the social model of disability rather than the medical model of disability.
- Learning about support models and resources.
- Understanding the importance of student and family relationships.

(Cologon, 2019, p. 50)

Teacher educators need to address these key elements as teachers have the unique opportunity to include or exclude students. Teachers create the culture of belonging and inclusion in their classrooms. Teacher preparation programs need to examine issues, biases, prejudices, and assumptions that teachers carry into the classroom and how these inform and influence teaching practice (Rose, 2002). The need for further research to ultimately improve the outcomes of inclusive education approaches will now be discussed.

Future recommendations

To date, limitations of research investigating evidence of inclusive education outcomes for students on the autism spectrum include: difficulties being able to make comparisons between and across settings; a limited quantity and quality of research; a lack of adequate measures; a lack of consistent use of measures; limited scope and sample size; as well as different contextual and school factors influencing the conclusions that can be drawn (Ferraioli & Harris, 2011). However, research conducted to date helps to identify what further research is needed to provide a larger and more consistent bank of evidence supporting inclusion of students on the spectrum. The research reported in this book highlights how the social and cultural context of education communities is important and that educators, families and students need to work together in respectful ways to support inclusion and a sense of belonging for all.

> ...*educators, families and students need to work together in respectful ways to support inclusion and a sense of belonging for all.*

It is important for research to help assist school communities to promote ethical leadership, build school capacity to implement inclusive practices, school connectedness, and ongoing support for professional learning to help build teacher confidence and self-efficacy. In addition, research that promotes whole-school and individual approaches to supporting student wellbeing, positive behaviour support, and the implementation of flexible and individual tailored approaches to programming and support is important (Saggers et al., 2018). Access to multidisciplinary support to help school communities make informed decisions about the type of support delivered is also essential (Saggers et al., 2018). Research can help inform what further changes to school environments may be needed, what further support schools and staff may require, what outcomes may be useful to measure, and what tools can be used as predictors of positive outcomes to ensure more accurate and extensive evidence can be gathered. The current paucity of research emphasises the continued need for further research focusing on how well inclusive education policies are being translated into inclusive practice. This will in turn allow for opportunities to capture evidence supporting inclusive education for students on the autism spectrum and more effectively measure outcomes (Sansosti & Sansosti, 2012).

Note

1 https://sustainabledevelopment.un.org/post2015/transformingourworld

References

Ainscow, M. (2007). Towards a more inclusive education system: Where next for special schools? In R. Cigman (Ed.), *Included or excluded? The challenge of the mainstream for some SEN children* (pp. 128–139). London: Routledge.

Ashburner, J., Ziviani, J., & Rodger, S. (2010). Surviving in the mainstream: Capacity of children with autism spectrum disorders to perform academically and regulate their emotions and behavior at school. *Research in Autism Spectrum Disorders*, 4(1), 18–27. doi:10.1016/j.rasd.2009.07.002.

Australian Government. (2005). *Disability Standards for Education 2005*. Canberra: Australian Government.

Australian Government. (2018). *Disability Discrimination Act 1992*. Canberra: Australian Government.

Australian Institute of Health and Welfare (AIHW). (2017). *Autism in Australia*. Australian Government. Retrieved from https://www.aihw.gov.au/reports/disability/autism-in-australia/contents/autism.

Beutel, D., Tangen, D., & Carrington, S. (2019). Building bridges between global concepts and local concepts: Implications for inclusive education in Nepal, Sri Lanka, & Bangladesh. *International Journal of Inclusive Education*, 23(1), 109–124. doi:10.1080/13603116.2018.1514763.

Biklen, D. (1988). The myth of clinical judgment. *Journal of Social Issues*, 44(1), 127–140. doi:10.1111/j.1540-4560.1988.tb02053.x.

Carrington, S. (1999). Inclusion needs a different school culture. *International Journal of Inclusive Education*, 3(3), 257–268. doi:10.1080/136031199285039.

Carrington, S., & Kimber, M. (2020). Ethical leadership for inclusive schools. *The Australian Educational Leader*, 42(2), 10–14.

Carrington, S., & MacArthur, J. (Eds.). (2012). *Teaching in inclusive school communities*. Brisbane: John Wiley & Sons.

Carrington, S., Mann, G., & Mavropoulou, S. (2019). *The existing inclusive education policy and inclusive education strategic plan in the Republic of Maldives*. Brisbane: Queensland University of Technology. Retrieved from https://eprints.qut.edu.au/135228/.

Cole, S., Murphy, H., Frisby, M., Grossi, T., & Bolte, H. (2019). *A longitudinal study to determine the impact of inclusion on student academic outcomes*. Centre on Education and Lifelong Learning, Indiana University. Retrieved from https://www.iidc.indiana.edu/styles/iidc/defiles/CELL/Inclusion-study-handout.pdf.

Cologon, K. (2013). *Inclusion in education: Towards equality for students with disability*. Melbourne: Children with Disability Australia.

Cologon, K. (2019). *Towards inclusive education: A necessary process of transformation*. Melbourne: Children and Young People with Disability Australia.

de Bruin, K. (2019). The impact of inclusive education reforms on students with disability: An international comparison. *International Journal of Inclusive Education*, 23(7–8), 811–826. doi:10.1080/13603116.2019.1623327.

Duke, J., Pillay, H., Tones, M., Nickerson, J., Carrington, S., & Ioelu, A. (2016). A case for rethinking inclusive education policy creation in developing countries. *Compare*, 46(6), 906–928. doi:10.1080/03057925.2016.1204226.

Ehrich, L. C., & Carrington, S. (2018). Making sense of ethical leadership. In J. Harris, S. Carrington, M. Ainscow, B. Comber, L. C. Ehrich, V. Klenowski, J. Smeed, & N. Spina, *Promoting equity in schools: Collaboration, inquiry and ethical leadership* (pp. 121–141). Oxon: Routledge.

Eldar, E., Talmor, R., & Wolf-Zukerman, T. (2010). Successes and difficulties in the individual inclusion of children with Autism Spectrum Disorder (ASD) in the eyes of their coordinators. *International Journal of Inclusive Education*, 14(1), 97–114. doi:10.1080/13603110802504150.

Estes, A., Rivera, V., Bryan, M., Cali, P., & Dawson G. (2011). Discrepancies between academic achievement and intellectual ability in higher-functioning school-aged children with autism spectrum disorder. *Journal of Autism and Developmental Disorders*, 41(8), 1044–1052. doi:10.1007/s10803-010-1127-3.

Ferraioli, S., & Harris, S. (2011). Effective educational inclusion of students on the autism spectrum. *Journal of Contemporary Psychotherapy*, 41(1), 19–28. doi:10.1007/s1087 9-010-9156-y.

Hansen, J. H., Carrington, S., Jensen, C. R., Molbæk, M., & Schmidt, M. C. S. (2020). The collaborative practice of inclusion and exclusion. *Nordic Journal of Studies in Education Policy*. doi:10.1080/20020317.2020.1730112.

Harris, A., & Jones, M. (2018). Why context matters: A comparative perspective on education reform and policy implementation. *Educational Research for Policy and Practice*, 17, 195–207. doi:10.1007/s10671-018-9231-9.

Hehir, T., Grindal, T., Freeman, B., Lamoreau, R., Borquaye, Y., & Burke, S. (2016). *A summary of the evidence on inclusive education*. São Paulo: Alana Institute.

Hehir, T., & Katzman, L. I. (2012). *Effective inclusive schools designing successful schoolwide programs*. San Francisco, CA: Jossey-Bass.

Hemmings, B., & Woodcock, S. (2011). Preservice teachers' views of inclusive education: A content analysis. *Australasian Journal of Special Education*, 35(2), 103–116. doi:10.1375/ajse.35.2.103.

Humphrey, N., & Symes, W. (2013). Inclusive education for pupils with autistic spectrum disorders in secondary mainstream schools: Teacher attitudes, experience and knowledge. *International Journal of Inclusive Education*, 17, 32–46. doi:10.1080/13603116.2011.580462.

Iadarola, S., Hetherington, S., Clinton, C., Dean, M., Raeisinger, E., Huynh, L., … Kasari, C. (2015). Services for children with autism spectrum disorder in three, large urban school districts: Perspectives of parents and educators. *Autism*, 19, 694–703. doi:10.1177/1362361314548078.

Jackson Brewin, B., Renwick, R., & Schormans, A. (2008). Parental perspectives of the quality of life in school environments for children with Asperger Syndrome. *Focus on Autism and Other Developmental Disabilities*, 23, 242–252. doi:10.1177/1088357608322997.

Jones, C. R., Happe, F., Golden, H., Marsden, A. J., Tregay, J., Simonoff, E., … Charman, T. (2009). Reading and arithmetic in adolescents with autism spectrum disorders: Peaks and dips in attainment. *Neuropsychology*, 23(6), 718–728. doi:10.1037/a0016360.

Jordan, A., Glenn, C., & McGhie-Richmond, D. (2010). The supporting effective teaching (SET) project: The relationship of inclusive teaching practices to teachers' beliefs about disability and ability, and about their roles as teachers. *Teaching & Teacher Education*, 26(2), 259–266. doi:10.1016/jtate.2009.03.005.

Jordan, R. (2008). Autistic spectrum disorders: A challenge and a model for inclusion in education. *British Journal of Special Education*, 35(1), 11–15. doi:10.1111/j.1467-8578.2008.00364.x.

Keen, D., Webster, A., & Ridley, G. (2015). How well are children with autism spectrum disorder doing academically at school? An overview of the literature. *Autism*, 20(3), 276–294. doi:10.1177/1362361315580962.

Kenny, L., Hattersley, C., Molins, B., Buckley, C., Povey, C., & Pellicano, E. (2016). Which terms should be used to describe autism? Perspectives from the UK autism community. *Autism*, 20(4), 442–462. doi:10.1177/1362361315588200.

Kozleski, E., Artiles, A., & Waitoller, F. (2014). Equity in inclusive education: A cultural historical comparative perspective. In L. Florian (Ed.), *The SAGE handbook of special education* (pp. 231–249). London: SAGE.

Lindsay, G., Ricketts, J., Peacey, L. V., Dockrell, J. E., & Charman, T. (2016). Meeting the educational and social needs of children with language impairment or autism spectrum disorder: The parents' perspectives. *International Journal of Language & Communication Disorders*, 51(5), 495–507.

Locke, J., Shih, W., Kretzmann, M., & Kasari, C. (2016). Examining playground engagement between elementary school children with and without autism spectrum disorder. *Autism*, 20(6), 653–662. doi:10.1177/1362361315599468.

Mayton, M. (2004). The quality of life of a child with Asperger's Disorder in a general education setting: A pilot case study. *International Journal of Special Education*, 20, 85–101.

Miles, M. (2013). *Buddhism and responses to disability, mental disorders and deafness in Asia*. Independent Living Institute. Retrieved from http://www.independentliving.org/miles2014a.

Oliver, M. (1996). *Understanding disability: From theory to practice*. Basingstoke: Macmillan.

Osborne, L. A., & Reed, P. (2011). School factors associated with mainstream progress in secondary education for included pupils with Autism Spectrum Disorders. *Research in Autism Spectrum Disorders*, 5(3), 1253–1263. doi:10.1016/j.rasd.2011.01.016.

Queensland Government. (2018). *Policy: Inclusive education*. Brisbane: Department of Education, Queensland Government.

Reed, P., & Osborne, L. (2014). Mainstream education for children with autism spectrum disorders. In J. Tarbox, D. R. Dixon, P. Sturmey & J. L. Matson (Eds.), *Handbook of early intervention for autism spectrum disorders: Research, policy, and practice* (pp. 447–485). New York, NY: Springer.

Roberts, J., & Simpson, K. (2016). A review of research into stakeholder perspectives on inclusion of students with autism in mainstream schools. *International Journal of Inclusive Education*, 20(10), 1084–1096. doi:10.1080/13603116.2016.1145267.

Rose, S. (2002). Inclusion and exclusion: An introduction. In R. Holdsworth (Ed.), *Who's in? Who's out? Issues of inclusion and exclusion in education policy. 2002 Applied educational policy seminar group* (Chapter 1) [Online]. Melbourne: Education Faculty, The University of Melbourne.

Ruijs, N. M., & Peetsma, T. T. D. (2009). Effects of inclusion on students with and without special educational needs reviewed. *Educational Research Review*, 4(2), 67–79.

Saggers, B., Campbell, M., Dillon-Wallace, J., Ashburner, J., Hwang, Y., Carrington, S., & Tones, M. (2017). Understandings and experiences of bullying: Impact on students on the autism spectrum. *Australasian Journal of Special Education*, 41(2), 123–140. doi:10.1017/jse.2017.6.

Saggers, B., Hwang, Y.-S., & Mercer, L. (2011). Your voice counts: Listening to the voice of high school students with autism spectrum disorder. *Australasian Journal of Special Education*, 35(2), 173–190.

Saggers, B., Klug, D., Harper-Hill, K., Ashburner, J., Costley, D., Clark, T., … Carrington, S. (2018). *Australian autism educational needs analysis: What are the needs of schools, parents and students on the autism spectrum?* Brisbane: Cooperative Research Centre for Living with Autism (Autism CRC).

Saggers, B., Tones, M., Dunne, J., & Aberdein, R. (2019). Tele-classroom consultation: Promoting an inclusive approach to supporting the needs of educators, families and early years learners on the autism spectrum in rural and remote areas in contextually responsive ways. *International Journal of Inclusive Education.* doi:10.1080/13603116.2019.1609103.

Saggers, B., Tones, M., Dunne, J., Trembath, D., Bruck, S., Webster, A., ... Wang, S. (2019). Promoting a collective voice from parents, educators and allied health professionals on the educational needs of students on the autism spectrum. *Journal of Autism and Developmental Disorders*, 49(9), 3845–3865. doi:10.1007/s10803-019-04097-8.

Sansosti, J., & Sansosti, F. (2012). Inclusion for students with high-functioning autism spectrum disorders: Definitions and decision making. *Psychology in the Schools*, 49, 917–931. doi:10.1002/pits.21652.

Segall, M., & Campbell, J. (2012). Factors relating to education professionals' classroom practices for the inclusion of students with autism spectrum disorders. *Research in Autism Spectrum Disorders*, 6, 1156–1167. doi:10.1016/j.rasd.2012.02.007.

Subba, A. B., Yangzom, C., Dorji, K., Choden, S., Namgay, U., Carrington, S., & Nickerson, J. (2019). Supporting students with disability in schools in Bhutan: Perspectives from school principals. *International Journal of Inclusive Education*, 23(1), 42–64. doi:10.1080/13603116.2018.1514744.

Szumski, G., Smogorzewska, J., & Karwowski, M. (2017). Academic achievement of students without special educational needs in inclusive classrooms: A meta-analysis. *Educational Research Review*, 21, 33–54. doi:10.1016/j.edurev.2017.02.004.

UNESCO. (2017). *A guide for ensuring inclusion and equity in education.* Paris: United Nations Educational, Scientific and Cultural Organization.

United Nations. (2006). *Convention on the rights of persons with disabilities.* New York, NY: United Nations.

United Nations. (2016). *Convention on the rights of persons with disabilities: General comment no. 4. Article 24: Right to inclusive education.* Geneva: United Nations.

Waddington, E., & Reed, P. (2006). Parents' and local education authority officers' perceptions of the factors affecting the success of inclusion of pupils with autistic spectrum disorders. *International Journal of Special Education*, 21, 138–150.

Whitaker, P. (2007). Provision for youngsters with autistic spectrum disorders in mainstream schools: What parents say – and what parents want. *British Journal of Special Education*, 34, 170–178.

Yumak, N., & Akgul, E. (2010). Investigating elementary school administrators' and teachers' perceptions on children with autism. *Procedia – Social and Behavioral Sciences*, 2, 910–914. doi:10.1016/j.sbspro.2010.03.125.

2
INCLUSIVE RESEARCH PRACTICE

Engaging autistic individuals and their families in research

Wenn B. Lawson and Suzanne Carrington

> Having presented the research evidence for inclusive education in Chapter 1, this chapter continues to apply the values of inclusion, this time to the research process. Inclusive research practices are based on the premise that the lived experiences of autistic individuals and their families provide them with unique expertise and perspective and therefore they should be included in the research that will affect them. This chapter aims to provide useful information for researchers who want to work in inclusive ways and increase community involvement. The first author of the chapter, Dr Wenn B. Lawson, who is himself on the autism spectrum, provides personal reflections, anecdotes, and examples which are threaded throughout the narrative in italicised text. The narrative provides clear direction about how researchers can engage and partner with individuals on the autism spectrum and families throughout the research process. Further to this, we discuss how to facilitate research groups with individuals on the autism spectrum, and how to report research results to individuals and families. Specific guidance includes how to recruit and retain research participants in longitudinal studies, evaluation of research outcomes and impact, and ideas about disseminating and utilising findings. The co-presentation of findings by researchers and individuals on the spectrum is addressed. Drawing on personal research experiences, this chapter guides researchers committed to conducting impactful research that translates to better outcomes for the autistic community.

In the past, much psychiatric and neurodevelopmental research about autistic people could be viewed as based in a deficit view of autism (Milton, 2014) that perpetuates marginalisation, stigma, and dependence. For example, some autism research was framed as searching for a cure which assumed that autism is a disease (Jaarsma & Welin, 2012). This view of autism is aligned with the medical model of disability that was discussed in Chapter 1. It is now understood that autism is not a disease but has been described as a different way of being human (Grinker, 2008; Prizant, 2015). 'Children with autism aren't sick; they are progressing through development stages as we all do. To help them, we don't need to change them or fix them. We need to work to understand them, and then change what we do. In other words, the best way to help a person with autism change for the better is to change ourselves – our attitudes, our behaviour, and the type of support we provide' (Prizant, 2015, p. 4). As Prizant reminds us, we need to listen to children, their parents, and autistic adults.

Researchers may perceive that they are engaged with the autistic community (Pellicano, Dinsmore, & Charman, 2014), but autistic people and their families have a different perspective and do not always trust researchers or their ways of translating knowledge from their research (Milton, Mills, & Pellicano, 2014). This could be due to a lack of interactional expertise with autistic communities and a lack of understanding and respect for their realities (Milton, 2014). When Temple Grandin published her first book in 1986, there were few autistic individuals who had described their own life in their own words. Her book, *Emergence: Labeled Autistic*, shared her experiences of being a child and an adult. She wrote about how she perceived and thought about the world, including her sensory sensitivities and shared her challenges of growing up. These stories contributed to a better understanding of and respect for autism (Grandin & Scariano, 1986).

Since that time, there has also been a growing public awareness and acknowledgement that the research community should be engaging with the autistic community as research partners to conduct research that will benefit them the most (Wynne, 2006). 'Taking autistic testimony seriously' (Jaswal & Akhtar, 2019, p. 12) indicates that it is time that researchers acknowledge the necessity of listening to autistic people about their experiences. An approach where researchers work directly with the autistic community will ensure that there is a better opportunity to know and understand autism (Pellicano, den Houting, du Plooy, & Lilley, 2019).

> ...the research community should be engaging with the autistic community as research partners to conduct research that will benefit them the most

Parents have also contributed to a better understanding of autism and have influenced research through their own fundraising for autism research (Silverman & Brosco, 2007). Parents' authority and participation in research is critical, particularly in the education context. Parent–teacher relationships have long been discussed as having a positive impact (Pushor, 2015) and research partnerships with parents can help educators have some understanding of what life is like with an autistic child. Rozanna Lilley is an anthropologist and education researcher who has a son on the autism spectrum. Her research (2013) documents experiences of mothers enrolling children diagnosed with autism in primary school and the narratives highlight feelings of exclusion and stigma. This type of research can have a positive impact on future educators because the research shares the experiences of real people. The challenge is to share research findings in ways that can really make a difference for the autistic community. Pellicano et al. (2019) argue that we need to change the way that research is conducted so that autistic people are meaningfully involved in all aspects of the research, including knowledge dissemination.

Autistic community engagement in research

In the areas of health and education, there has been a growing expectation that researchers work in respectful and participatory ways with autistic individuals and their families. Participatory research varies and may include the autistic community working as consultants, advisors, or collaborators in research planning, data collection, analysis, and knowledge translation (Jivraj, Sacrey, Newton, Nicholas, & Zwaigenbaum, 2014). The *Participatory and Inclusive Autism Research Practice Guides (Version 3)* (Autism CRC, 2020a) highlight that an important element of participatory research is the consideration of power which is about the influence and control that an autistic person may have in the research process. The *Participatory and Inclusive Autism Research Practice Guides (Version 3)* (Autism CRC, 2020a) describe different levels of participation that range from 'coercing' which is controlled by an academic, right up to 'community led' and 'community control' where the autistic community has control. The levels of community participation may also reflect positions of power. For example, coercing is about being forced into doing something and feeling patronised, and the levels that support an autistic community-led and -controlled approach are about getting the help that is needed and will make a difference. Research co-production with the autistic community is at the higher level of the participatory approach hierarchy and is dependent on joint initiation, development, and implementation of research through to joint data analysis and sharing of the findings. This approach is seen as the most effective way to ensure research impact (Jung, Harrow, & Pharoah, 2012).

> *In the areas of health and education, there has been a growing expectation that researchers work in respectful and participatory ways with autistic individuals and their families.*

Taking an inclusive approach to research means that the autistic community is engaged in research that will improve the lives of families and individuals. It is suggested that knowledge is more likely to be useful, applicable, and impactful if the autistic community is engaged in the research in meaningful ways (Pellicano et al., 2019). This means that researchers need to consider the planning and conducting of research that is driven by the needs of the autistic community rather than the researchers themselves. In Australia, the Cooperative Research Centre for Living with Autism (Autism CRC) has committed to inclusive and participatory autism research and has implemented strategies to encourage research co-production and reframe the direction of research based on stakeholders' needs and values. The following section will provide an overview of the practice guides that have informed an inclusive approach to research in the Autism CRC.

The *Participatory and Inclusive Autism Research Practice Guides*

These practice guides and checklists were developed to support the aims of the Autism CRC to transform lives of autistic people by engaging in collaborative end-user research. It is clear that these guides and checklists set a high standard for autism research by acknowledging that autistic people are the true experts in their field (Autism CRC, 2020a). The practical resources were developed by autistic researchers, researchers not on the spectrum, and adults on the spectrum and were informed by research. The third version was produced in 2020 and has a focus on the elements of participatory research, building relationships with community stakeholders, and sharing power between academic and non-academic stakeholders.

The key message is that there is a new approach for conducting autism research. The *Participatory and Inclusive Autism Research Practice Guides* (Autism CRC, 2020a) suggest that researchers should be aiming for the highest level of community participation that can be achieved and provide practical ideas to plan participatory research that considers the power between researchers and the autistic community. A detailed framework for a partnership process covers the partnership stage (engagement; formalisation; mobilisation; and maintenance) and the research stage (commissioning research; undertaking research; and disseminating, evaluating, and utilising research) (Autism CRC, 2020a). The *Participatory and Inclusive Autism Research Practice Guides* provide detailed and practical information to support each step of participatory research.

The Autism CRC also instigated The Research Program (formerly known as the Research Academy) offered by the Sylvia Rodger Academy, which trained a group of researchers and people on the spectrum in co-production (Autism CRC, 2020b). Many of the graduates from the Academy are now working in research co-production in Autism CRC-funded projects.

The following parts of the chapter explore ideas about engaging autistic participants in autism research including co-production, with consideration being given to the cognitive, emotional, physical, and relational needs for all concerned. The first author of the chapter, Dr Wenn B. Lawson, who is himself on the autism spectrum, provides personal reflections, anecdotes, and examples which are threaded throughout the narrative (see italicised text integrated throughout the rest of the chapter). As an expert on his own experiences, his comments provide an insider account of involvement in autism research and as a person on the autism spectrum. He also highlights the need for describing the research purpose in detail, and why this might need to be carried out differently to that for an individual not on the spectrum. Attention is given to facilitating research groups that incorporate individuals and families, as well as various ways to report research results. Specific guidance will include how to recruit and retain autistic individuals as research participants in longitudinal studies. The evaluation of research outcomes and impact, and ideas about disseminating and utilising findings, will also be outlined.

Engaging autistic people as research participants

Engaging autistic individuals as participants in research isn't as simple as handing out a flyer, posting an advertisement on social media, or even passing the desire for people to respond to a research project by word-of-mouth. Although these mediums might work in a limited way, they fail to consider how autism impacts the learning and understanding of autistic people, how this is different even among the autistic community, and how this knowledge needs to guide the engagement of autistic participants.

> Engaging autistic individuals as participants in research isn't as simple as handing out a flyer, posting an advertisement on social media, or even passing the desire for people to respond to a research project by word-of-mouth.

Therefore, before engaging autistic participants, the cognitive style (how they access and process information) needs to be understood. Autistic people use attention (the needed resource to notice something) quite differently to those not on the spectrum (e.g., Happé & Frith, 2006; Lawson, 2011). This might mean that reaching autistic people in order to share a research idea or project may require consideration of how their interest is triggered, how they learn, and how they process information. For example, some autistic people may notice another's intention (read their words and/or gestures) and, therefore, they can predict an outcome. Most autistic people, however, will have difficulties with this ability due to poor object permanence (e.g., see Lawson & Dombroski, 2017), poor interoceptive connection (e.g., see Goodall, 2019), and being very much 'one tracked or single focused' in their processing and experience (e.g., see Lawson, 2011). *Therefore, our subsequent culture will likely be less inclusive of small talk and of social 'niceties'.*

Sensory distraction

Sensory distraction is important to appreciate because it impacts how autistic people 'reach out' to individuals, how they phrase information being given, and how they respond to feedback.

> *Because communication in autism tends to be of a literal nature, you might need to avoid using metaphorical components in your delivery of a research project idea. Also, autism only allows for attention to single foci at any one time, rather than multiple foci. So expecting an autistic individual to listen might mean you need to keep your hands still, avoid wearing strong perfumed deodorants and so on, as well as avoiding the use of jewellery, bright coloured clothing, or/and any other suspect 'things' that might capture attention and take away from the message you need to share.*

So, as part of the autistic cognitive style, having good eye contact, using considered 'appropriate' facial expression, and showing 'appropriate' reading of body language and connected interoceptive awareness (e.g., Lawson, 2011; Lawson & Dombroski, 2017) may not happen as expected in and by people who are not autistic or may happen at a reduced level.

Body language

In the communication experience for people who are not on the autism spectrum, it is expected others will 'read between the lines', use lots of facial expressions and body language to help boost the spoken word, and give reassurance of the verbal conversation. However, this is not the case in autism where words spoken may come from a voice without intonation, may not be accompanied by body language or facial expressions, and may give rise to a very 'black and white' translation (Lawson, 2000; Ramachandran, 2011; Williams, 1993). Therefore, being straightforward with autistic people generally works better than 'beating around the bush'.

Key components of engagement

With consideration of the above, engaging autistic people as participants takes two key components. The first one involves building an understanding for individuals of what the research is about and why we need to do it. This means writing up an explanation of what the research is about, what the process involves, and what the intended outcome might be. For many autistic people, having this information presented in writing is beneficial, but others will need it represented visually, by video, and even a mix of all of the above. However, because we are all more different than we are alike, there is no one way that works for all. *Please ask us what might work best for us!*

The second part of this process of engagement will take trust. Autistic people will need to build a relationship with those individuals they are hoping to share with in the research project (Gowen et al., 2019; Pellicano et al., 2014). Unfortunately, many autistic people have a very negative and even traumatic experience of partaking in research. For some, it has caused them to feel '*like guinea pigs*' and robbed them of a sense of value. Rather than feeling like individuals of value, with insider knowledge and experience to share, they may have felt like a number, devoid of their humanity.

> *For example, during a five-day Research Academy upskilling event where autistic adults came together to share in a co-production training residential, several of the adults told stories of their experiences being a research participant. As they shared their stories with us, there were many tears and much grief. This was due to feeling 'damaged' by researchers who hadn't responded ethically to them, hadn't fulfilled a commitment to them, and/or hadn't treated them in respectful ways. The first day of our co-production residential was spent rebuilding bridges and repairing what we could of the hurt and pain caused by previous researchers. So, without a sense of trust in you, as a researcher, autistic participation may be elusive.*

Therefore, a consideration of the individual autistic cognitive style and a trust relationship between the researcher and the participant are mandatory.

> *For me, as well as being very singly focused, my processing style means I need to talk things over to gain an understanding of content. It's as I talk over things with another that I uncover connections to understanding and I can make sense of the conversation. Simply giving me a document to read may not be adequate. Also, I can't talk and take notes; it's one or the other.*

This might mean a need to record a conversation so that the participant can re-listen to it, or it might mean the other person takes notes and then shares them with the autistic participant.

Coexisting conditions

As well as autism having an impact upon cognitive style, autism tends to operate with a variety of 'cousins'. For example, according to some researchers (e.g., Panagiotidi, Overton, & Stafford, 2017; Stevens, Peng, & Barnard-Brak, 2016), Attention Deficit with Hyperactivity Disorder (ADHD) accompanies autism in 14–85% of instances. It is certainly commonly known that autism implies a shorter attention span, without interference from any cousins. Again, this knowledge, if relevant, will impact upon the type(s) of conversations a researcher has with a potential participant, for example: short, punchy, to the point, while individuals move around on their chair, rock, play with a sensory toy and so on (compared to expectations of those not on the spectrum, or ADHD individuals whose attention may wander). Other autistic individuals may show a lack of movement or body affect, and a stilted monotone conversational manner. Some autistic people are dyslexic, dyspraxic, and/or live with hypermobility and fatigue. These all commonly co-occur with autism and will impact the communication process.

It may be considered impolite to ask an individual about their history when researchers are looking for autistic people for their research project; however, they will need to know this. They will need to know about their diagnostic status, if they have any mental health or sensory issues that could impact how they partake in any research processes, what, if any, coexisting conditions they have, and if they are available for either the short or long term. Defining short and long term will be important because they may have differing ideas about what might be meant by these. *For example, I can remember being told to 'stop talking' but no-one explained how long 'stop' was to last for.*

Research clarity and expectations

The purpose for the research needs clear definition. This may sound obvious; however, sometimes what can appear clear to a person who is not on the autism spectrum is very confusing for an autistic person.

> *For example, I remember being told that I would receive a phone call and this would give myself and the other person a time to chat over things together. I waited*

> *in all evening for that phone call! Oh, the time that might have been saved if I could have been given an expected time frame! On another occasion I was told there would be a time to chat together over a Skype call. The date and time were set but, at that time, I didn't know what a 'Skype call' was. I simply expected my phone to ring at that time. The thing is, if I don't know that I don't know something, then I don't know that I don't know! So, I can't check in on my understanding.*

The research purpose needs to be laid out simply and clearly. Saying, for example, that the research is exploring 'sleep' among the autistic population does not specify whether or not individuals sleep on their side or on their back. If the research is exploring if autistic individuals need as much sleep as individuals who are not autistic, what might impact sleep quality (e.g., anxiety, diet), or what might aid sleep in autism (e.g., listening to music or a podcast as a person goes to sleep, watching television as they go to sleep, having a warm bath or going for a walk, and so on), then this needs to be spelled out.

Autistic people may frequently say 'yes' to things asked of them because they can do them. However, this isn't the same as actually doing them.

> *For example, if asked, 'Can you run a focus group?', I may respond, 'Yes, I can'. 'Can you', is not the same as: 'OK, you said you can run a focus group, that's great. Can you run a focus group with these eight people at Rose's home on July 15, 2021 and explore their thoughts, ideas and suggestions about their experience of employment as younger adults?'*

An autistic person may need time to process questions like this, and a way to check in with the researcher on how to get more information, such as: 'Who in the group will be the scribe?', 'Who will record the minutes?', 'Who will lead the group or am I expected to be the facilitator?', or 'How will I share information from this group with you?'

In cases where a research project is longitudinal and will require a participant to be available for, for example, the next five years, this will need to be stated up front. *As autistic people, we value being valued!* This will mean lots of following up with participants via texts, phone calls, emails, and so on. Some researchers will find it difficult to set boundaries (your time, my time, shared time), but it is vital that this is made clear. Sometimes the definitions of 'colleague', 'co-worker', or 'friend' will need clarifying, and sometimes more than once.

> *When I was a young adult I thought if someone introduced themselves to me and called me by my name, we were friends. I believed I should be able to contact this person at any time of day or night. I didn't understand the boundaries that I needed to respect and felt personally affronted when someone said they couldn't talk to me because they were with their friends or family – after all I was a friend!*

Recruiting and retaining individuals can be a different experience for autistic individuals when compared to individuals who are not on the spectrum. For example, some autistic people won't talk over the telephone while others will only talk over the phone. It is important to ask questions and establish preferences so that individual participants know what to expect from the other. For example, during the recruitment phase, it may be necessary to word research participant requests to include how they might prefer to be contacted, as well as by what means, what times, and if they will be in need of a support person during the process.

Value, value, value

It is important to let an individual know the key role they play in the research, and that their needs are valued. This might include what they need during this process, and the understanding that their needs may change with time. There needs to be emphasis on the idea that what they say and how they are involved is as important as the ways they will be kept informed. Value in who they are and how they are involved is extended all the way through the research project (name the points/phases for when this will occur and notify in writing of any changes to this timetable). It is a case of equal participation and equal value throughout the research project.

> *It is important to let an individual know the key role they play in the research, and that their needs are valued.*

This research isn't being done on you, about you, or for you but it's being done together with you. This always reminds me of the saying: 'don't walk behind me or in front of me, walk with me'. This of course implies the person needs to adjust their stride to fit in with mine.

Other considerations

Facilitating research groups with individuals on the autism spectrum might involve a different process than that needed for people who are not on the spectrum. It is often taken for granted that a group or gathering for research purposes may have several people (usually up to 12) meeting in a room, on the same night, and at the same time. Autistic individuals may not have employment during the day, but they may be very tired during the evening. Therefore, they may be less likely to have '*enough spoons*' for the energy needed to be part of a group meeting that takes place in the evening, or that takes place in a physical setting with others.

Therefore, a focus group may be more successful when conducted over Zoom or Skype. Having a virtual gathering allows individuals to move around, get a comfortable space that is familiar to them, and removes the pressures associated with travel, unfamiliarity, and so on. Most individuals who are going out to an office space or community place for a meeting take time to shower, plan their time and their trip, and take care of any mealtime needs. All of these actions require attention which could mean, for an autistic person, less available attention for the actual meeting. It is important to remember that autistic people are '*mono*' (having single attention available via one channel at any one time) people, not '*poly*' (able to shift and share attention between channels at a multi-task level) people. So, all that extra attention given to dress code, travel, meals, time, and coping with the sensory attacks coming from other people (their hair, their after shave, their movements, etc.) can rob autistic people of needed energy and time to share within a group meeting.

> *Partnering with individuals and families in research could look and feel different for autistic individuals.*

Partnering with individuals and families in research could look and feel different for autistic individuals. One strategy that can support any given partnership is the use of shared interest. In many ways, it is easier for a person who is not autistic to join the autistic interest, rather than the other way around. Therefore, if you build a trust relationship, you will get to know what a person's likes and dislikes are. What is it that motivates them? It is true we all learn and function best when we are interested in something; however, autistic people actually find it very difficult to 'connect' or attend to something outside of their interest. There is research to demonstrate autistic people function best when motivated (see Koegel, Kim, Koegel, & Schwartzman, 2013; Lawson, 2013) and can be unavailable to notice or attend if not interested. On the other hand, people who are not autistic have no difficulty either aligning their interests with others or feigning interest when they are not interested (Murray, Lesser, & Lawson, 2005).

Termination

It is not uncommon (due to literality and an all or nothing disposition) that if an autistic person feels unheard, not valued, and so on, they may pull the plug and terminate the relationship. To keep the relationship going well, it is therefore important to check in frequently, check their perceptions of how things are doing, and keep the relationship fluid. It will also be important that participants understand that any project they might be involved with, will end. Often when there has been such an intense connection, there will be a need to curve the contact slowly and make sure there are ongoing supports in place that individuals can utilise when the project finishes (or beforehand if needed).

Families

Families wanting to do the very best for their autistic family member can easily speak on their behalf. Although it is important to hear their voice, it is even more important to hear the voice of the autistic person, unless the research project is focused on the experience of the wider family. The perspective of either the nuclear or extended family, especially if they are not autistic, will obviously be different to that of the autistic individual. So, although of equal value, these differences will need to be accommodated, especially in the light of the understanding of the differing cognitive styles between autistic populations and populations of those who are not autistic. Also, autism is highly genetic (e.g., Bai et al., 2019) so it is possible that another family member (parent, sibling) may be somewhere on the autism spectrum. Knowing what we do about cognitive style in autism and sensory dispositions, as well as associated 'cousins', it will be important to account for these within the wider family partnerships in research.

How to report research results to individuals and families will very much depend upon the relationships within the family, the age and culture of the family members, as well as the wider family culture. Some might request one copy of results be made available to the family to share, but others will want their own copy. Making research reports accessible to autistic individuals their families and the wider community will mean presenting those findings in different formats. This can vary from simply a written report, graphs and tables, pie charts, and other visual representation of the data, right through to a video recording of the same information but with more emphasis upon the visual dynamics. There are also a number of software packages that allow data to be presented in a variety of formats, also creating much more accessibility for a wider variety of differing access needs.[1]

How to co-produce research

Co-production of research means jointly working together: co-production is not just a word; not just a concept; it is a meeting of minds, a coming together to find a shared solution. In practice, it involves people who use services being included and working together from the start to the end of any project that affects them. There are various research concepts, the most known are:

- Traditional methodology: One researcher plus multiple subjects. The researcher instructs subjects, collects data from subject performance, analyses the data, and informs the discussion from the analysed results.
- Participatory methods: Focus groups and multi-stakeholder meetings, participatory inquiry, action research, oral testimonies and story collection as a foundation for collective analysis, photo-digital stories, photo-voice, drawing and essay writing competitions, participatory video, and immersions.

In co-produced research, participants influence the research agenda, the process, and actions. Researchers and participants share the power and control throughout the research process. The process is not dominated by any one person, but all are in it together – from agreement on the topic to research, to methods for enquiry, to the process of acquisition and analysing the data, to actioning any outcomes – it's *all* a joint affair. The research process may involve researchers who may or may not be autistic, and autistic people such as students, parents, and teachers. No one person has power over another. For example, autistic researchers come in all shapes and sizes. Some may be verbal and interactive. Some may be quiet and need time to think and process. All, however, have a wealth of knowledge and experience to share in ways that suit them. Each will bring perspectives to enrich the research process in ways that only autistic researchers can do. This gives authenticity and credibility to the work in ways not available if they are not included.

What co-production isn't

Co-production isn't one person's idea that others are invited to share in some aspects of, but is delegated by the boss. It isn't involving another person in the beginning but not fully keeping them in the loop. It isn't any one person concluding that certain individuals don't need to be involved in everything. Co-production isn't sharing a research project proposal, then staying on board together through the project but not sharing in the finished product. Co-production acknowledges that different people have different roles in the research and that each person's role will depend on their individual knowledge, skills, and experience (Tritter & McCallum, 2006).

Partnerships

Can a partnership be a partnership if it's not equal? Can there be equality between autistic people and people who are not autistic? It is important to think how we can ensure an 'equal' partnership, then make it happen.

> As an autistic person, like other autistic people, I have an uneven profile of ability. I love writing and research but I am slow to process information. My uneven skills can shake my confidence. Taking time together, autistic people and those who are not autistic alike, to share together those things we each find threatening to our abilities would help level the playing field somewhat.

For autistic people to be fully included in any co-produced research, we must make time for processing and for creating inclusive opportunities, environments, and plans together around how to make it happen.

Some ideas that might help:

1. We might prefer to read ahead of any meetings.
2. We might prefer to join with others over Skype or Zoom.
3. We might work best when we don't attend with others, therefore we need to think of alternatives.
4. We need to facilitate co-production via accommodating individual needs (sensory, processing time, etc.)
5. Sometimes it's hard to 'notice' when others are attempting to tell me something, like 'my time to talk' or 'time for you to stop'. I might need support with this.

6. *I use a speaking clock on my laptop monitor because I'm not likely to notice someone putting up a hand or notice for time to stop.*
7. *We also need to think about what the most comfortable circumstances for the whole team might be.*

Building capacity in a powerless population?

Many autistic people are used to having others make decisions for them. They are too often referred to by way of their 'deficits'. As autistic people, their skills and strengths are undervalued and under employed. *Take time, work with us to enable 'healing' from hurt and pain.* This foundation begins restorative structures leading to co-produced participatory credible research.

Reflections

We conclude this chapter with our own personal reflections. Interacting with each other as co-authors has provided us with an opportunity to learn from each other and to make a contribution to autistic research. Ultimately we want to see autistic people and researchers working in partnership to conduct meaningful research that has a positive impact and leads to better outcomes for the autistic community.

Wenn B. Lawson: *Working on this chapter together with Suzanne started from the right premise, for me. I'm very thankful Suzanne's request for me to contribute was supported by the clarity of what she wanted from me. This included not just the what, but also the 'how'. I knew I could Zoom and connect digitally, by email or phone and so on. All mediums were equally valued.*

I do much better when requests are structured and set out in ways that are clearly defined, with clear boundaries and clear beginnings and clear endings (such as titles to write or work with, particular information requested or required to research and word limits).

I also value being valued! Sometimes, because my autism imposes limits upon my attention, energy levels, and processing style, I can become very negative about my ability. This can rob me of good self-esteem. Having Suzanne request that I share in the writing of this chapter emphasised, despite some of the disabling aspects of being autistic, we can navigate these together. When others make appropriate accommodations, the knowledge and ability autistic people possess will positively contribute to our shared understanding.

Suzanne Carrington: *It has been a great learning experience for me to work with Wenn B. Lawson. We worked as partners and divided the writing into sections with word limits to enable us to meet our goal. We worked on numerous drafts with emails going back and forth, always checking in on each other and how we were feeling about life in general! I began with the overview of the literature that informs our argument and then Wenn shared insights from his own experience as an autistic researcher and member of the autistic community.*

I found the headings that Wenn provided such as sensory distraction, body language, key components of engagement, coexisting conditions, and research clarity and expectations as wonderful organisers to guide my own thinking and understanding. Wenn's personal quotes provide real examples that helped me to value autism and the autistic perspective in ways that would not have been possible if I was just reading a list of research tips. I really want to thank Wenn for working with me on this chapter.

Note

1 See, for example: https://ckan.org/; https://www.vic.gov.au/make-content-accessible; https://www.capterra.com/sem-compare/data-visualization-software?gclid=EAIaIQobChMIp9KEwKiC6gIVxH0rCh2AnAO0EAAYAiAAEgJL6_D_BwE

References

Autism CRC. (2020a). *Participatory and inclusive autism research practice guides (Version 3)*. Brisbane: Cooperative Research Centre for Living with Autism (Autism CRC).

Autism CRC. (2020b). *Sylvia Rodger Academy*. Retrieved from https://www.autismcrc.com.au/sylvia-rodger-academy.

Bai, D., Yip, H., Windham, G. C., Sourander, A., Francis, R., Yoffe, R. ... Sandin, S. (2019). Association of genetic and environmental factors with autism in a 5-country cohort. *JAMA Psychiatry*. doi:10.1001/jamapsychiatry.2019.1411.

Goodall, E. (2019). *Understanding the autism spectrum*. Government of South Australia. Retrieved from https://www.education.sa.gov.au/sites/default/files/understanding-the-autism-spectrum.pdf?acsf_files_redirect.

Gowen, E., Taylor, R., Bleazard, T., Greenstein, A., Baimbridge, P., & Poole, D. (2019). Guidelines for conducting research studies with the autism community. *Autism Policy & Practice*, 2(1 A new beginning), 29–45.

Grandin, T., & Scariano, M. (1986). *Emergence: Labeled autistic*. Novato, CA: Arena Press.

Grinker, R. R. (2008). *Unstrange minds: Remapping the world of autism*. New York, NY: Basic Books.

Happé, F., & Frith, U. (2006). The weak coherence account: Detail-focused cognitive style in autism spectrum disorders. *Journal of Autism and Developmental Disorders*, 36(1), 5–25.

Jaarsma, P., & Welin, S. (2012). Autism as a natural human variation: Reflections on the claims of the neurodiversity movement. *Health Care Analysis*, 20, 20–30.

Jaswal, V. K., & Akhtar, N. (2019). Being versus appearing socially uninterested: Challenging assumptions about social motivation in autism. *Behavioural and Brain Sciences*, 42(e82), 1–14. doi:10.1017/S0140525X18001826.

Jivraj, J., Sacrey, L., Newton, A., Nicholas, D., & Zwaigenbaum, L. (2014). Assessing the influence of research–partner involvement on the process and outcomes of participatory research in autism spectrum disorder and neurodevelopmental disorders: A scoping review. *Autism*, 18(7), 782–793.

Jung, T., Harrow, J., & Pharoah, C. (2012). *Co-producing research: Working together or falling apart?* CGAP Briefing Note 8, January 2012. London: Centre for Charitable Giving and Philanthropy.

Koegel, R., Kim, S., Koegel, L., & Schwartzman, B. (2013). Improving socialization for high school students with ASD by using their preferred interests. *Journal of Autism and Developmental Disorders*, 43(9), 2121–2134. doi:10.1007/s10803-013-1765-3.

Lawson, W. (2000). *Life behind glass*. London: Jessica Kingsley Publishers.

Lawson, W. (2011). *The passionate mind: How individuals on the autism spectrum learn*. London: Jessica Kingsley Publishers.

Lawson, W. (2013). Sensory connection, interest/attention and gamma synchrony in autism or autism, brain connections and preoccupation. *Medical Hypothesis*, 80(3), 284–288.

Lawson, W., & Dombroski, B. (2017). Problems with object permanence: Rethinking traditional beliefs associated with poor theory of mind in autism. *Journal of Intellectual Disability – Diagnosis and Treatment*, 5(1), 1–6. doi:10.6000/2292-2598.2017.05.01.1.

Lilley, R. (2013). It's an absolute nightmare: Maternal experiences of enrolling children diagnosed with autism in primary school in Sydney, Australia. *Disability & Society*, 28(4), 514–526. doi:10.1080/09687599.2012.717882.

Milton, D. (2014). Autistic expertise: A critical reflection on the production of knowledge in autism studies. *Autism*, 18(7), 794–802.

Milton, D., Mills, R., & Pellicano, L. (2014). Ethics and autism: Where is the autistic voice? Commentary on Post et al. *Journal of Autism and Developmental Disorders*, 44, 2650–2651. doi:10.10007/s10803-012-1739-x.

Murray, D. M., Lesser, M., & Lawson, W. (2005). Attention, monotropism and the diagnostic criteria for autism. *Autism*, 9(2), 139–156.

Panagiotidi, M., Overton, P. G., & Stafford, T. (2017). Co-occurrence of ASD and ADHD traits in an adult population. *Journal of Attention Disorders*, 23(12), 1407–1415. doi:10.1177/1087054717720720.

Pellicano, E., den Houting, J., du Plooy, L., & Lilley, R. (2019). Knowing autism: The place of experiential expertise. *Behavioural and Brain Sciences*, 42. doi:10.1017/S0140525X18002376.

Pellicano, E., Dinsmore, A., & Charman, T. (2014). Views on researcher–community engagement in autism research in the United Kingdom: A mixed-methods study. *PLoS ONE*, 9(10). doi:10.1371/journal.pone.0109946.

Prizant, B. M. (2015). *Uniquely human: A different way of seeing autism*. New York, NY: Simon & Schuster.

Pushor, D. (2015). Walking alongside: A pedagogy of working with parents and family in Canada. In L. Orland-Barak & C. J. Craig (Eds.), *International teacher education: Promising pedagogies (Part B)* (pp. 233–251). Bingley: Emerald Group Publishing Limited.

Ramachandran, V. S. (2011). *The tell-tale brain: A neuroscientist's quest for what makes us human*. New York, NY: W. W. Norton & Company.

Silverman, C., & Brosco, J. P. (2007). Understanding autism: Parents and pediatricians in historical perspective. *Archives of Pediatrics & Adolescent Medicine*, 161(4), 392–398.

Stevens, T., Peng, L., & Barnard-Brak, L. (2016). The comorbidity of ADHD in children diagnosed with autism spectrum disorder. *Research in Autism Spectrum Disorders*, 31, 11–18.

Tritter, J. Q., & McCallum, A. (2006). The snakes and ladders of user involvement: Moving beyond Arnstein. *Health Policy*, 76(2), 156–168.

Williams, D. (1993). *My experience with autism, emotion and behaviour* [Documentary aired on Eye to Eye with Connie Chung, USA].

Wynne, B. (2006). Public engagement as a means of restoring public trust in science – Hitting the notes, but missing the music? *Community Genetics*, 9, 211–220.

PART 2
Outcomes of an inclusive research approach

Birds of Differences (by Toby Prendergast, aged nine years)

'*I like drawing birds and mixing textures to create art. Birds are clever as they see treasures where humans see rubbish. So each bird has found a treasure of autism which has given me strength.*'

3

SUPPORTING STUDENTS ON THE AUTISM SPECTRUM IN INCLUSIVE SCHOOLS

Research to inform implementation of support and evidence-based practices

Beth Saggers and Suzanne Carrington

> Research that includes a range of stakeholder groups, including students on the spectrum and their families, provides rich and uniquely insightful data to support inclusion and inclusive practices in school communities. This chapter reports on the first completed research project in the School Years Program of the Cooperative Research Centre for Living with Autism (Autism CRC): the *Australian Autism Educational Needs Analysis* (ASD–ENA). This research produced the first Australia-wide needs analysis of students on the spectrum (aged 5–18 years). The survey collected information from four key participant groups nationwide in Australia: educators, specialist support staff, parents of students on the spectrum, and students themselves (aged 11–18 years). Educators, specialists, families, and students all emphasised the need for social emotional learning and support as a foundation for all learning at school. Results particularly highlighted the importance of school connectedness, student retention, participation, and engagement with a focus on flexible and individually tailored educational approaches to programming and support. Based on participants' views, the findings from this survey informed much of the subsequent work in the School Years Program and provide insight into what is needed to support inclusive approaches in school communities.

It is well understood that inclusive education is about all students learning together. Access to the standard curriculum, participation in school and classrooms in respectful ways with peers, and support from teachers working with specialists where needed contribute to an inclusive model of education. The key message is that we are all different and we all belong. Autistic students may present unique challenges to school systems and an inclusive approach to education requires teachers to address these challenges and support the unique needs of these students.

Globally, the number of children being diagnosed on the autism spectrum has increased substantially over the past three decades (Baio et al., 2018). Furthermore, some research suggests that children on the spectrum are increasingly being educated in inclusive settings (Ravet, 2011; Roberts & Simpson, 2016; Saggers, Tones, Dunne, Trembath, et al., 2019). However, there is also research evidence as discussed in Chapter 1 indicating that this group of students continues to be segregated and that there is an urgent need to support staff to implement inclusive practices that can adequately support this group of students in inclusive ways (de Bruin, 2019). Despite a growing body of research investigating inclusive education outcomes and the successful participation, engagement, and learning of students on the autism spectrum, this group of students continues to be susceptible to poorer educational outcomes than other students (Ashburner, Ziviani, & Rodger, 2010; Jones et al., 2009; Keen, Webster, & Ridley, 2015; Roberts & Simpson, 2016). Moreover, effective support to adequately meet the educational needs of students on the spectrum continues to be recognised by all stakeholders (including educators, parents, specialists, and students) as a key challenge to success (Saggers, Tones, Dunne, Trembath, et al., 2019).

> The key message is that we are all different and we all belong.

It is important, therefore, that research focuses on developing not only a better understanding of the needs of this particular group of students but also identifies the needs of the educational communities by recognising factors that challenge or enable schools to successfully meet these needs. This type of research, which takes a multiple stakeholder view, can also give us a better insight into how well research and inclusive policies are being translated into practice and can help inform what more is needed from research, policy, and practice points of view to support educational communities and help them mobilise and translate research knowledge (Roberts & Simpson, 2016; Saggers et al., 2018; Saggers, Tones, Dunne, Trembath, et al., 2019). Informed by this type of multiple stakeholder needs analysis research, an integrated approach to inclusion as described by Ravet (2011) can then bring together a rights- and needs-based perspective to inclusion in order to identify distinct pedagogies based on individual student needs that maximise the success of all students in inclusive settings (Ravet, 2011; Saggers, Tones, Dunne, Trembath, et al., 2019).

One method that is often used to explore multiple stakeholders' perspectives in research is to conduct a needs assessment or analysis. A needs analysis has been described by Powers and Knapp (2010) as using a 'problem-solving process for the purpose of collecting, organising, and presenting information that describes the needs of a target population and evaluates their importance relative to demand' (p. 120). This type of research can be a vehicle to ensuring the voice of *all* stakeholders is heard and that important messages from different stakeholders are identified and acknowledged and inform research and practice (Grimshaw, Eccles, Lavis, Hill, & Squires, 2012; Saggers et al., 2018; Saggers, Tones, Dunne, Trembath, et al., 2019;

Soriano, 2013). This approach can also help to nurture a collective voice or view on the topic of research interest that can further promote the success of knowledge translation (Saggers, Tones, Dunne, Trembath, et al., 2019). The research discussed in this chapter adds to the growing body of research evidence collected from the perspectives of multiple stakeholders (Pellicano, Bölte, & Stahmer, 2018; Pellicano, Dinsmore, & Charman, 2014; Roberts & Simpson, 2016). The researchers conducted a nationwide needs analysis to get a better understanding of the educational needs of students on the autism spectrum from multiple stakeholder perspectives. The details of this research project will now be discussed.

Overview of the research project

One foundational piece of research conducted as part of the Autism CRC has been the *Australian Autism Educational Needs Analysis: What are the Needs of Schools, Parents and Students on the Autism Spectrum?* (ASD–ENA; Saggers et al., 2018). The overarching aim of the research was to collect the perspectives of a range of different stakeholders (educators, specialists, parents, and students on the spectrum) through a needs analysis to get a better understanding of the educational needs of students on the spectrum, but in turn also identify enablers and challenges to education communities in meeting these needs. The results of this type of research can, as previously described, be used to bring together a rights- and needs-based perspective to inclusion (Ravet, 2011; Saggers, Tones, Dunne, Trembath, et al., 2019) that can be used to identify distinct pedagogies to maximise the success of students on the spectrum in inclusive settings and support knowledge translation in policy and practice for educational communities.

The research aimed to examine, on a nationwide scale, the collective voice of key stakeholders including students on the spectrum, in the hope of developing a more accurate profile of the education support needs of students on the spectrum. Also profiling strategies that are commonly implemented with this group of students to gain a better understanding of the enablers and challenges for educational communities in supporting the educational needs of students on the spectrum in educational contexts.

This type of research is informed by a range of different end-users and has clear outcomes for knowledge translation and informing future inclusive research, policy, and practice. It can also help to identify the professional learning needs of different stakeholder groups and challenges to implementation of research-informed practices within the context of school communities. It is this type of real-world research informed by the multiple perspectives from people in the field and the 'autistic' community that can promote successful inclusive outcomes. This type of research ensures the voices of people on the ground at the coal face of inclusion in action are heard. It enables researchers, families, and practitioners to come together to identify in an evidence-based way what works, what does not work, what more is needed to support successful inclusion, as well as what enables or hinders the translation of research knowledge and policies into practice within individual contexts.

The Autism CRC School Years Program of research had a focus on a broad range of research methodologies and included school-based and participatory research. Our research approach valued the voice of the autistic community and the educators, families, and specialists who provided support. Our vision was to conduct research that delivered results and outcomes that make a difference and have a positive impact in schools. This particular study gave many people a voice about what was needed to support education for students on the autism spectrum and has informed a range of practical resources that support an inclusive approach. These resources are shared on *inclusionED*,[1] the community web platform for educators. *inclusionED* is the knowledge translation tool for the School Years Program in the Autism CRC and will be discussed in more detail in Chapter 5. Feedback from educators about the needs analysis research has indicated that this research is meaningful and relevant to the education community. This is reflected in the following comment one educator shared:

> Awesome job in doing research to actually find out what it is that these kids need! I'm very disheartened ... resources and staffing keeps getting CUT rather than increased ... classroom staff are too overloaded ... they don't have the time to undertake their own training in their own time.

The aims of the research were to identify:

1. What key stakeholders perceive are the educational needs of students on the spectrum (aged 5–18 years), particularly those with high impact social, emotional, behavioural, and complex needs.
2. What key stakeholders perceive are the supports required to successfully meet the educational needs of students on the spectrum (aged 5–18 years), particularly those with high impact social, emotional, behavioural, and complex needs within school settings.
3. What key stakeholders perceive are the enablers and challenges to implementing appropriate support and strategies to meet the needs of students on the autism spectrum.

Methodology

Method

The needs analysis used a mixed methods sequential explanatory design (Cameron, 2009; Creswell, 2012; Ivankova, Creswell, & Stick, 2006) to collect data across two sequential phases. Phase 1 involved participation from key stakeholders (including educators, specialists, parents, and students on the spectrum aged 11–18 years) in a nationwide survey that involved the use of both quantitative Likert scale questions as well as qualitative open-ended questions. After the survey closed, a random selection of participants who had indicated an interest were invited to be involved in follow-up semi-structured interviews (Phase 2). The interviews provided the opportunity to gain further information to extend the breadth and depth of survey findings (Driscoll, Appiah-Yeboah, Salib, & Rupert, 2007).

Participants and recruitment

There were four key participant groups that were the focus of recruitment for the research. These included:

1. Parents of school-aged students on the autism spectrum aged 5–18 years of age.
2. Educators of students on the autism spectrum (e.g., administration, class teachers, and ancillary staff) who were involved in or had previously been enrolled in the education of school-aged students on the autism spectrum.
3. Specialist educators and allied health professionals working in schools (e.g., education specialists, allied health professionals, psychologists) who were working or had previously worked to support school-aged students on the autism spectrum.
4. Students on the autism spectrum (aged 11–18 years).

Actioning a research project that was on such a large scale was a world first and was both challenging and daunting in size, complexity, and timeframes. The research presented challenges in not only developing a nationwide recruitment strategy but also in recruiting and collecting data from multiple stakeholders and across a range of different education systems and ethical processes nationally. The research was therefore not without its pitfalls and limitations.

Phase 1

A nationwide recruitment strategy, employing a purposive sampling technique (Patton, 2002), was used to recruit participants from every state and territory in Australia. The first step in this strategy was to identify as many relevant organisations, people, and support groups that could be considered representative of the stakeholder groups as possible. Some examples included 'parent-based organisations and support groups, autism-specific organisations, educational organisations, professional organisations and networks, researcher networks, and social networking groups (Twitter and Facebook)' (Saggers, Tones, Dunne, Trembath, et al., 2019, p. 3847). Information about the study was then disseminated through these organisations, groups, and individuals and generally occurred through a range of electronic means and via social media (e.g., emails, word of mouth, radio interviews, conferences, email signatures, flyers, and advertising on key websites). In total, 99 national and state-based organisations were approached (generally with an information flyer and link to the survey) and asked to distribute the survey among their members. In total, out of the 99 organisations approached, 33 organisations agreed to distribute the information, 12 of these were nationally based organisations with the other 21 being state-based. To get the maximum uptake possible, response rates from different areas were monitored and a repeat, more targeted selective sampling recruitment strategy was implemented in areas where the response rate was low using the techniques described above.

Phase 2

Participants could indicate their interest to be involved in the Phase 2 follow-up semi-structured interviews and provide their contact details for this purpose at the end of the Phase 1 survey. A random selection of ten individuals from each participant pool was then selected and invited to be involved in the Phase 2 interviews.

Development of Phase 1 surveys

Four customised surveys (one for each participant group) were designed to ensure that the survey adequately reflected the different roles and perspectives of the participants in meeting the needs of students on the spectrum. The surveys included both quantitative Likert scale questions and open-ended qualitative questions. 'The experience and knowledge base of a multidisciplinary research team informed development of survey questions' (Saggers, Tones, Dunne, Trembath, et al., 2019, p. 3848) and survey questions were designed based on the core features of the autism spectrum (American Psychiatric Association [APA], 2013) and findings from the Australian Advisory Board on Autism Spectrum Disorders (AABASD) position paper (2012) which highlights eight educational principles for school-aged Australian students on the spectrum (see below and Saggers, Tones, Dunne, Trembath, et al., 2019):

1. Every child and adolescent on the spectrum should have access to an educational service appropriate to his her/needs.
2. All government and non-government educational sectors should provide educational services that cater to the needs of children and adolescents on the spectrum.
3. Educational services must be responsive to all children and adolescents across the spectrum.
4. There should be a range of educational services for children and adolescents on the spectrum.
5. Educational services must address the students' needs in communication, social skills, learning, sensory issues, and behaviour and include family involvement.
6. Increased provision of teacher education and training to improve the capacity of educational services to provide for students on the spectrum.
7. Educational services are based on sound evidence and quality indicators.
8. Following an application for service, enrolments should proceed in a timely manner to ensure students on the spectrum access appropriate educational services as soon as possible.

Each survey was piloted with suitable participants who volunteered to provide feedback in consultation with an autism organisation involved in the research and the feedback was used to further refine the survey. Each of the four surveys included questions relative to that participant group on key topics such as:

- Demographics.
- School needs (academic, social emotional, communication).
- Sensory needs.
- Behavioural and mental health needs.
- Transition needs.
- School connectedness.
- Use of technology.
- Support needs.
- Experiences including remote consultative approaches.

The open-ended questions on the survey gave participants opportunities to expand upon their responses.

Participants could self-select which participant group they wished to complete a survey for, and surveys took approximately one hour to complete. This stage of the project was exceptionally challenging with each different stakeholder survey having to be developed to not only reflect the different role of the stakeholders, but to also reflect differences in education systems nationally and the education of different age groups. The student survey was quite different to other surveys in order to reflect the unique role of the student in the education process.

Phase 2 interviews

The semi-structured interviews further explored stakeholder perceptions and expanded on results of the survey with a focus on obtaining more information on 'needs for which students on the spectrum required most support in school settings, most commonly implemented supports, and factors that facilitated or inhibited providing support' (Saggers, Tones, Dunne, Trembath, et al., 2019, p. 3848). Follow-up interviews took approximately 20–30 minutes to complete.

Data analysis

Descriptive analysis of quantitative data was conducted on appropriate variables extracting frequencies, percentages, and mean scores. A thematic approach was applied to analysis of the qualitative data collected through open-ended questions and interviews (Braun & Clarke, 2019).

We have outlined the methods used to obtain vital information on the needs of students on the spectrum in inclusive schools, and we now turn to the key findings from the data. This was a significant milestone in the project and it was challenging to be able to not only clean but analyse the data and be able to get to this point.

Key findings of the research

According to participants, the learning needs of students on the spectrum that had the most impact on learning and participation and required the most support, accommodations, and adjustments were linked to the key core features of the autism spectrum. One educator commented:

> I think that schools need to learn that inclusion is not just allowing a child on the campus, it is much more and needs to be a collaborative and involved process ... All students have a value and a future that is worth our time.

All participant groups (educators, specialists, parents, and students) identified social emotional needs as having the most impact on their learning and academic success and required the most additional support in learning contexts (Saggers et al., 2018; Saggers, Tones, Dunne, Trembath, et al., 2019). An often-overlooked aspect of schools is the strong social elements of learning in this environment that underpins everything. Schools are very complex, social environments, and social environments that are extremely dynamic, organic, and fluid in nature with the social dynamics often changing or evolving depending on who you are interacting with within these environments and for how long. This was reflected in one parent's comment:

> *All participant groups (educators, specialists, parents, and students) identified social emotional needs as having the most impact on their learning and academic success and required the most additional support in learning contexts*

> He's actually quite gifted in academics but he has a lot of social issues, particularly as he gets into the higher grades and as social interaction becomes a lot more intricate ... He really needs a much higher level of support socially and emotionally as opposed to probably learning.

Other areas of need that had the most impact included the behavioural, communication, and sensory needs of students on the spectrum. Interestingly, the participants rated the academic and learning needs of students on the spectrum as having the least impact of all their needs and required the lowest levels of support, assistance, adjustment, or accommodation. Participants felt it was the other needs described that had the most impact on learning. There was also strong agreement among participants that the sensory experiences that had the greatest impact on students learning in the school environment were related to noise. This was followed by touch and having to sit still (Saggers et al., 2018). This was reflected by this educator who stated:

> It's knowledge and skills and it's about the science of autism and the science of teaching ... really looking at evidence-based practice and what works for our young people so that they can (a) engage in learning ... Then (b) get on with the job of learning.

Participants also had the opportunity to consider the behavioural and mental health needs of this group of students. Overall, the students themselves reported issues with mental health and wellbeing as very high. Of the 107 students who participated in the study, 94% reported clinically significant difficulties with their mental health and wellbeing with substantial risk of emotional and peer problems. One student stated:

> I made it through primary school only because of Mrs N. She taught me strategies to deal with my emotions, while always supporting me. She knew how to teach me how to calm down. She was understanding. She would advocate for me to other teachers at the school.

Almost half the students had an additional diagnosis of anxiety disorders, almost a quarter had an additional diagnosis of depression, and almost a quarter also had an additional diagnosis of social emotional disorder. Overall, on the student-reported wellbeing measures, 93.5% of the students indicated they experienced depression and 87% experienced moderate levels of negative mood, with 73% experiencing negative self-esteem. In addition, one third of the group reported high levels of separation anxiety, social phobia, and generalised anxiety. In addition, tasks that students rated as most difficult to deal with in schools included the social demands such as working as part of a group and coping with bullying and teasing as well as emotional regulation including managing their anxiety and staying calm. Other stakeholders' responses also recognised supporting the social elements of school and managing anxiety as critical to success in this environment. These results strongly corroborated all stakeholders' views that it was the social emotional needs of students on the spectrum which needed the most support in schools and had the biggest impact on learning and academic success (Saggers et al., 2018).

Other elements of the school environment that students rated as most difficult were related to:

- The need for proficient use of executive function skills (e.g., planning for assignments and doing homework, organising self and thoughts, attention to task).
- Issues related to handwriting (e.g., being neat, being quick enough to keep up, and copying information from the board).
- Coping with change.

One student described the difficulties they have as:

> I get into trouble all the time at school for things I can't control talking loud getting too close to other people interrupting. I don't mean to do this stuff my brain just does it. I hate my brain.

When students were asked what were helpful strategies that could support the difficulties they had identified with the learning environment, several key findings were reported:

- Using technology (e.g., to support academic work and handwriting).
- Support with executive function skills (e.g., organisation and planning of themselves, school tasks, belongings).
- Social support (e.g., to manage social situations and bullying).

- Emotional regulation (e.g., to manage anxiety).
- Transition support (e.g., warning of impending change).
- Assessment adjustments (e.g., extra time, quiet space, scribe, homework).
- Personnel support (e.g., time away, one-on-one support, extra help).
- Special interests (e.g., to support learning and as rewards).
- Rewards (e.g., recognition of things done well).
- Visual supports (e.g., copies of information).

One student stated:

> The most helpful thing is a good teacher who can write clear instructions … The most important thing I get is help to be organised at home with my books, timetable and homework.

Parents, educators, and specialists all identified the importance of a positive approach to behaviour support in schools as essential to an inclusive approach. Four key challenges to meeting some of the more complex needs of students were identified by stakeholders as: i) funding; ii) lack of time; iii) lack of suitable education and training; and iv) lack of specialist support (Saggers et al., 2018).

> *Parents, educators, and specialists all identified the importance of a positive approach to behaviour support in schools as essential to an inclusive approach.*

Other findings reflected the importance of supporting all transitions and having suitable transition planning strategies in place, as transitions can take up to 25% of anyone's day. In addition, aligned with supporting social emotional wellbeing was the need to promote school connectedness, with students on the spectrum scoring very low on school connectedness scores, demonstrating a limited sense of belonging to their school community. Furthermore, the importance of an integrated use of technology to support all aspects of learning was highlighted (Saggers et al., 2018).

The research findings reported in this chapter have been well received by educators, parents, and the autistic community. This is evidenced by the number of visits and comments on the Autism CRC Facebook pages where various resources such as Powtoons, infographics, and PowerPoint summaries of the research have been shared. In addition, there have been many invitations to speak at education conferences to share the findings and resources that are the outcomes of this research. The various resources that have been developed from this project and are available on *inclusionED* will also inform teacher and specialist preparation for supporting education for students on the spectrum.

Progressing inclusive education

Education systems around the world, including in Australia, have their own policies to support inclusive practice and outline how the policies impact on teaching, resource allocation, and leadership to support quality education for all students (UNESCO, 2015).

Further to our focus on translating the knowledge from this research, we also strive to engage with our education partners to inform education policy that will be incorporated into new models of inclusive practice. Policy enactment (Ball, Maguire, & Braun, 2012) is not well understood and has not been well documented in the area of inclusive education (Massouti, 2018). The enactment of policy requires an assemblage of people who implement practices and plans and use materials in various ways (Riveros & Viczko, 2016). This is particularly relevant for education where school principals, teachers, and specialists are working with parents and students in different contexts to progress inclusive education.

However, when governments implement new education policy, there may be little democratic engagement and discussion with the people, the teachers, and school leaders who will be putting the policy into practice (Werts & Brewer, 2015). It is clear that in education, context impacts on how policy is enacted in practice (Massouti, 2018). If there is an expectation of change to more inclusive practice, then contextual factors such as the beliefs and values of teachers and school leaders, their motivations, and the capacities that educators may have to implement an inclusive approach need to be taken into consideration.

In Chapter 1, we discussed the models of disability and emphasised the importance of the social model of disability (Oliver, 1996) as an underlying framework for inclusion. This model guides educators to consider aspects of the education system, the ways that teaching is provided, access to the curriculum, the organisation of the learning environment, and models of support that create barriers for students with disabilities to be included. An inclusive approach to education often requires a change in beliefs and attitudes to our understanding and expectations in education (Carrington, 1999). The key message from the Autism CRC School Years Program of research is to see diversity in students as a normal part of society and the school community. We suggest that the *Australian Autism Educational Needs Analysis* (ASD–ENA) findings and resources could support the development of educators' knowledge, confidence, and skills in supporting students on the autism spectrum to be successful at school in inclusive settings and influence beliefs and attitudes towards inclusion.

How does this research help inform practice?

What does this needs analysis research tell us about meeting the needs of students on the autism spectrum in inclusive settings? The first thing it tells us is that we are not there yet; that is, there continues to be significant issues and substantial challenges to meeting the needs of this group of students in school that we need to address to ensure inclusive practices adequately meet the needs of this population (Saggers, Tones, Dunne, & Aberdein, 2019).

The second thing it tells us is a collaborative, collective approach is needed involving the family, the student, and specialist and multidisciplinary input when necessary to support practices that are 'contextually fit' (Saggers et al., 2018; Saggers,

> *Sensory elements are also a key aspect of the learning environment that need to be considered and adjusted particularly in relation to noise, touch, and having to stay still*

Tones, Dunne, & Aberdein, 2019). It also tells us that this population needs inclusive practices that embed explicit, individualised support as needed that recognises and addresses the unique characteristics of students on the spectrum and that provides bespoke, flexible, individualised approaches in response. This was described by one specialist's comments:

> Professionals with specialist knowledge ... need to be working alongside the teachers and within the classrooms at school so that they can up-skill educators to better understand the sensory and communicative needs of these children ... Traditional behaviour management does not support the underlying emotional stress that these children undergo.

Parents also highlighted the importance of collaborating with families as highlighted by this parent's comment:

> Lots of communication between parents and staff. Parents know their children best and things can change quickly, ASD kids cover up a lot of emotions at school and let it out at home. Having an honest relationship because not everything the school does helps/works.

Critically, it informs us that the social emotional needs, wellbeing, and sense of belonging continue to be the *highest* priority for this group of students and will in turn also support their academic learning (Saggers, Tones, Dunne, Trembath, et al., 2019). In relation to student wellbeing, it is also essential to consider co-existing conditions experienced by students on the spectrum, particularly as they move into adolescence. An awareness of and support for anxiety, depression, attention difficulties, learning and communication issues, and auditory processing needs should be considered as part of an inclusive approach and draw on specialist support and multidisciplinary input as needed (Saggers et al., 2018). Sensory elements are also a key aspect of the learning environment that need to be considered and adjusted particularly in relation to noise, touch, and having to stay still (Saggers et al., 2018).

One parent described their child's social emotional needs:

> He doesn't want to be treated like a charity case and have his 'difference' constantly brought to people's attention, however the constant rejection by peers is debilitating. Even as a parent, I feel lonely and rejected – because my son is somehow invisible, so am I.

Furthermore, as part of an inclusive approach, building school capacity and improving awareness of a student's individual strengths and interests, as well as a focus on effectively supporting the unique needs of students on the spectrum, is key. This approach would involve the whole school as well as more individualised approaches and support implemented through a multi-tiered system of support that would also draw on specialist and multidisciplinary support as needed to implement informed approaches through this tiered system (Saggers et al., 2018). Positive behaviour support is a vital element to support this framework (Saggers et al., 2018). The importance of human and material resources to support inclusive practices should not be overlooked.

Another key element of inclusive practices that can be drawn from this research is the importance of educational approaches as discussed in the needs analysis report (Saggers et al., 2018) that need to consider student preferences for support, including: using technology to support needs; provide more individualised support inside and outside the classroom when needed; support executive function, social, and sensory elements of school and transitions; as well as provide support for emotional regulation and handwriting.

In relation to the professional learning of educators and specialists working in inclusive settings, a focus on teacher confidence and self-efficacy in supporting students on the spectrum is essential. Educators and specialists stated that they preferred professional learning through a combination of face-to-face professional development training, seminars, professional support methods (e.g., coaching), and observations of others' practice online. Most importantly, teachers need support in situ to ensure professional learning can be translated into contextually appropriate strategies (Saggers, Tones, Dunne, & Aberdein, 2019). The first author of this book chapter was project leader of this research and now reflects on experiences of leading this research retrospectively.

Researcher reflection on the research

I feel that a needs analysis approach that includes the voice of all stakeholders is an essential first step that is often not taken or is underutilised in research. If we are to be truly inclusive, the importance of promoting a collective, collaborative voice from all stakeholders should not be underestimated in research (Saggers, Tones, Dunne, Trembath, et al., 2019). This research was a once in a lifetime chance to seek a collective view of the needs for this population. The research has been a great platform which has set the scene and formed the foundation for informed educational research within the School Years strand of the Autism CRC. Furthermore, it has informed research into other student populations both nationally and internationally. However, there are several limitations to this research, most of which were related to the constraints the restricted timeframes applied. These included limited time to develop research instruments, ethical constraints, missing data that had to be dealt with, and uneven representation amongst stakeholder groups, none of which are uncommon when doing this type of research on such a large scale with a very limited budget.

So, if I had my time over again as project leader, what would I do differently? Below I list a few things that come to mind:

- *More time to do the research; other needs analysis projects in other fields have completed what was done in 12 months in this research across three or four years and with larger budgets. More time would allow for:*
  - *Extended reach of recruitment strategies including social media.*
  - *More opportunity to get additional ethics approvals from state and commonwealth organisations so recruitment could have spread in breadth and depth across all regions and participant groups.*

- More opportunity to recruit larger numbers from all stakeholder groups nationwide.
- More opportunity to consult with the autism community about the survey tools and interview questions through their development and piloting, and to further refine the research instruments.
- More opportunity to conduct additional follow-up interviews and implement a range of different inclusive practices in collecting data that would provide further support to the autism community involved in the research.
- More time to analyse the data and work with the autism community to provide a shared view of results.

Note

1 www.inclusioned.edu.au

References

American Psychiatric Association (APA). (2013). *Diagnostic and statistical manual of mental disorders* (5th ed.). Arlington, VA: American Psychiatric Association.

Ashburner, J., Ziviani, J., & Rodger, S. (2010). Surviving in the mainstream: Capacity of children with autism spectrum disorders to perform academically and regulate their emotions and behavior at school. *Research in Autism Spectrum Disorders,* 4(1), 18–27. doi:10.1016/j.rasd.2009.07.002.

Australian Advisory Board on Autism Spectrum Disorders (AABASD). (2012). *Education and Autism Spectrum Disorders in Australia: The provision of appropriate educational services for school-age students with Autism Spectrum Disorders in Australia.* Position paper 2010, updated 2012. Sydney: Australian Advisory Board on Autism Spectrum Disorders.

Baio, J., Wiggins, L., Christensen, D. L., Maenner, M. J., Daniels, J., Warren, Z., ... Dowling, N. F. (2018). Prevalence of autism spectrum disorder among children aged 8 years: Autism and developmental disabilities monitoring network, 11 Sites, United States, 2014. *MMWR Surveillance Summaries,* 67(6), 1–23. doi:10.15585/mmwr.ss6706a1.

Ball, S. J., Maguire, M., & Braun, A. (2012). *How schools do policy: Policy enactments in secondary schools.* New York, NY: Routledge.

Braun, V., & Clarke, V. (2019). *Guidelines for reviewers and editors evaluating thematic analysis manuscripts.* Retrieved from https://cdn.auckland.ac.nz/assets/psych/about/our-research/documents/Checklist%20for%20reviewers%20and%20editors%20evaluating%20thematic%20analysis%20manuscripts.pdf.

Cameron, R. (2009). A sequential mixed model research design: Design, analytical and display issues. *International Journal of Multiple Research Approaches,* 3(2), 140–152.

Carrington, S. (1999). Inclusion needs a different school culture. *International Journal of Inclusive Education,* 3(3), 257–268.

Creswell, J. W. (2012). *Educational research: Planning, conducting, and evaluating quantitative and qualitative research.* Boston, MA: Pearson.

de Bruin, K. (2019). The impact of inclusive education reforms on students with disability: An international comparison. *International Journal of Inclusive Education,* 23(7–8), 811–826. doi:10.1080/13603116.2019.1623327.

Driscoll, D. L., Appiah-Yeboah, A., Salib, P., & Rupert, D. J. (2007). Merging qualitative and quantitative data in mixed methods research: How to and why not. *Ecological and Environmental Anthropology,* 3(1), 19–28.

Grimshaw, J. M., Eccles, M. P., Lavis, J. N., Hill, S. J., & Squires, J. E. (2012). Knowledge translation of research findings. *Implementation Science*, 7. doi:10.1186/1748-5908-7-50.

Ivankova, N.V., Creswell, J.W., & Stick, S. L. (2006). Using mixed methods sequential explanatory design: From theory to practice. *Field Methods*, 18(1), 3–20. doi:10.1177/1525822X05282260.

Jones, C. R., Happé, F., Golden, H., Marsden, A. J., Tregay, J., Simonoff, E., ... Charman, T. (2009). Reading and arithmetic in adolescents with autism spectrum disorders: Peaks and dips in attainment. *Neuropsychology*, 23(6), 718–728. doi:10.1037/a0016360.

Keen, D., Webster, A., & Ridley, G. (2015). How well are children with autism spectrum disorder doing academically at school? An overview of the literature. *Autism*, 20(3), 276–294. doi:10.1177/1362361315580962.

Massouti, A. (2018). (Re)thinking the adoption of inclusive education policy in Ontario schools. *Canadian Journal of Educational Administration and Policy*, 185, 32–44.

Oliver, M. (1996). *Understanding disability: From theory to practice*. Basingstoke: Macmillan.

Patton, M. Q. (2002). *Qualitative research and evaluation methods* (3rd ed.). Thousand Oaks, CA: Sage.

Pellicano, L., Bölte, S., & Stahmer, A. (2018). The current illusion of educational inclusion. *Autism*, 22(4), 386–387.

Pellicano, L., Dinsmore, A., & Charman, T. (2014). What should autism research focus upon? Community views and priorities from the United Kingdom. *Autism*, 18(7), 756–770. doi:10.1177/1362361314529627.

Powers, B. A., & Knapp, T. A. (Eds.). (2010). *Dictionary of nursing theory and research* (4th ed.). New York, NY: Springer.

Ravet, J. (2011). Inclusive/exclusive? Contradictory perspectives on autism and inclusion: The case for an integrative position. *International Journal of Inclusive Education*, 15(6), 667–682.

Riveros, A., & Viczko, M. (2016). The enactment of professional learning policies: Performativity and multiple ontologies. In M. Viczko & A. Riveros (Eds), *Assemblage, enactment and agency: Educational policy perspectives* (pp. 55–69). New York, NY: Routledge.

Roberts, J., & Simpson, K. (2016). A review of research into stakeholder perspectives on inclusion of students with autism in mainstream schools. *International Journal of Inclusive Education*, 20(10), 1084–1096. doi:10.1080/13603116.2016.1145267.

Saggers, B., Klug, D., Harper-Hill, K., Ashburner, J., Costley, D., Clark, T., ... Carrington, S. (2018). *Australian autism educational needs analysis: What are the needs of schools, parents and students on the autism spectrum?* Brisbane: Cooperative Research Centre for Living with Autism (Autism CRC).

Saggers, B., Tones, M., Dunne, J., & Aberdein, R. (2019). Tele-classroom consultation: Promoting an inclusive approach to supporting the needs of educators, families and early years learners on the autism spectrum in rural and remote areas in contextually responsive ways. *International Journal of Inclusive Education*. doi:10.1080/13603116.2019.1609103.

Saggers, B., Tones, M., Dunne, J., Trembath, D., Bruck, S., Webster, A., ... Wang, S. (2019). Promoting a collective voice from parents, educators and allied health professionals on the educational needs of students on the autism spectrum. *Journal of Autism and Developmental Disorders*, 49(9), 3845–3865. doi:10.1007/s10803-019-04097-8.

Soriano, F. (2013). *Conducting needs assessments: A multidisciplinary approach* (2nd ed.). Thousand Oaks, CA: SAGE.

UNESCO. (2015). *Education 2030 Incheon declaration and framework for action*. Paris: UNESCO.

Werts, A. B., & Brewer, C. A. (2015). Reframing the study of policy implementation: Lived experience as politics. *Educational Policy*, 29(1), 206–229. doi:10.1177/0895904814559247.

4
AUTISTIC VOICES IN AUTISM EDUCATION RESEARCH

Trudy Bartlett and Suzanne Carrington

> This is the final chapter in Part 2 that focuses on sharing the outcomes of an inclusive research approach. The research approach in the School Years Program has involved many voices of teachers, allied health professionals, parents, specialists from autism organisations, and students and young people on the autism spectrum. This chapter extends the focus in Chapter 2 by describing how an inclusive and participatory approach to research can support better outcomes for education if we want schools to be more responsive to the needs of autistic students and teachers. The first author of this chapter, Trudy Bartlett, is an autistic educator. Trudy tells her story about how she became involved in the Autism CRC and became a strong advocate for the research in the School Years Program. Trudy emphasises how listening to the voices of people on the autism spectrum can transform education research to be more participatory and inclusive. By listening to her story and key messages, researchers in this field can conduct more impactful research and make a positive difference to the lives of young people on the autism spectrum.

Over recent years, there has been a stronger focus on autism research that addresses the needs and realities of autism but also engages more collaboratively with the autistic community (Pellicano et al., 2018). Autistic people have been more involved as research participants, research partners, and as researchers themselves (Nicolaidis et al., 2019) and grant authorities now rightly expect researchers to plan for how the funded research will have an impact on policy and practice and translate to benefits for society. This translational approach to research is strongly aligned with the research to support inclusive education for students on the autism spectrum, as presented in this book.

In this chapter, we present our experiences and our ideas about why it is important to listen to the voices of autistic people if we want schools to be more responsive to the needs of autistic students and teachers. It is evident that school communities that value and respect their members, provide a safe learning environment for everyone to express their views, build awareness, and develop capabilities together are more likely to be inclusive (Carrington & Robinson, 2006). There are many examples in the research literature that describe how students have been valued and respected as citizens in their school communities (for example, see Carrington & Holm, 2005), and these types of approaches support a more respectful culture that can overcome the power relationships between teachers and students that create barriers to equity and inclusion.

> *It is evident that school communities that value and respect their members, provide a safe learning environment for everyone to express their views, build awareness, and develop capabilities together are more likely to be inclusive*

The shift in autism research highlights the response to criticisms of research about minority groups in general. As Raymaker and Nicolaidis (2013) explain, 'members of the minority community are typically seen by scientists as simply sources of raw data' (p. 171). 'Scientists who do not understand their subjects' cultural contexts or abilities are more likely to design faulty research methods and draw questionable conclusions from their data' (Raymaker & Nicolaidis, 2013, p. 173). In the case of autism research, clinicians and scientists may implement 'treatments', provide 'interventions', and gather data from the participants in the research. The use of language such as 'treatments' and 'interventions' highlights the medical approach that was discussed in Chapter 1 of this book and perpetuates the ableist enculturation in special education that may construct disabled people as tragic and pathologised (Watson, 2018). Research that evaluates the impact of 'treatments' and 'interventions' may also perpetuate existing power structures between researchers and people from the autistic community. There have been a range of research approaches that support respectful and collaborative ways of working and the next section of this chapter will present a brief overview of these approaches. They are:

1. Participatory research.
2. Voice research.
3. Co-production research.

Participatory research

Pellicano et al. (2018) describe participation as taking part in any or all parts of the research process – from being a research participant to being actively involved in the design. This research approach respects and values the perspectives and participation of the autistic community and moves away from the power dynamics of using autistic people as a source of data (Raymaker & Nicolaidis, 2013). Taking participatory research a step further, researchers can conduct participatory inquiries with community members as full members of the research team. This is called community-based participatory research (CBPR) (Israel et al., 2003).

Voice research

Researchers in areas such as health, education, and social services have an increasing focus on listening to the voices of children and adults who receive support. Organisations are seen to actively engage and consult, rather than make decisions on behalf of others (Long, Panese, Ferguson, Hamill, & Miller, 2017). Student voice or pupil voice is well known in education research (Rudduck & Flutter, 2004) and is informed by Article 12 of the UN *Convention on the Rights of the Child* (United Nations, 1989). The process of developing more inclusive and socially just schools requires a culture where people are valued and treated with respect for their varied knowledge and experiences (Carrington, 1999). Meaningful student involvement has been shown to be a powerful and effective force for school improvement (Rudduck & Flutter, 2004). Involving young people as researchers in their school communities positions youth as full research partners and values their knowledge and skills, as opposed to positioning them as participants in research (Carrington, Bland, & Brady, 2010).

> *Meaningful student involvement has been shown to be a powerful and effective force for school improvement*

Co-production research

Research co-production involves researchers and autistic people working together as peers and recognises and equally values the skills of researchers and the expertise that people on the autism spectrum and their families/carers have gained through their lived experiences (Autism CRC, 2020c). This type of approach supports outcomes that are meaningful and responsive to the needs of this population and supports learning about more respectful ways of thinking and practice for the broader research community. Autistic people can be engaged at every stage of the research process – from identification of research questions, data collection and analysis, through to dissemination and knowledge translation (Cargo & Mercer, 2008).

Inclusive research: Autism CRC

The approach taken by researchers in this book challenges and shifts the power relationships between researchers and the autistic community. It also highlights the value and respect that the researchers have for educators, families, and autistic students. The Autism CRC aims to transform lives through collaborative research with the autism community and those people and organisations who provide support. 'People on the autism spectrum need to be at the centre of everything we do' (Autism CRC, 2020b). In the School Years Program of research, individuals on the spectrum and their families have been involved in developing the research agenda, planning, implementing, and dissemination of research. This type of approach could be described as an inclusive research model (Walmsley & Johnson, 2003) because the autistic community are included in all phases of the research. In the Autism CRC, autistic people may engage with 'framing questions, providing input on research design, helping with research tasks such as providing input on survey readability/wording and accessibility, entering data, analysing data, providing input on interpretation of findings, co-writing and authoring papers and reports, and co-presenting research findings at meetings and conferences' (Autism CRC, 2016, p. 6).

The research reported in this book describes the participation of autistic children, young people, and adults and their families, as well as the participation of clinicians and educators. This approach is documented in the *Participatory and Inclusive Autism Research Practice Guides (Version 3)* (Autism CRC, 2020b). This resource is a practical resource that supports researchers to engage in co-production and meaningful engagement with autistic people. During the seven years of the Autism CRC research, the research leaders have worked to build research capacity within the autistic community and to build knowledge, awareness, and skills of the researchers to partner with the autistic community to co-produce research. The aim is to support impactful research that makes a difference in the lives of autistic people.

In the next section of this chapter, the first author shares her experiences as a teacher and her involvement in the Autism CRC research and leadership programs. Listening to autistic voice is emphasised as an important requirement of moving forward to a more inclusive approach to research that will truly make a difference for autistic people and their future success in education.

How I came to be involved with the Autism CRC

It was 2018 and I was in my first full-time leadership role in my teaching career. I had a negative experience with a colleague who was not supportive of my autistic ways of working. I was feeling that I could not use the supports that I needed to help manage my sensory needs in the school environment. This made it difficult for me to continue to work in that position and within that department.

As a result, I began to question my ability to be in a leadership role and if teaching was even the right job for me if I could not use my supportive strategies in the classroom. The doubt I developed in myself resulted in me leaving the position and questioning what other careers or jobs I could do other than teaching. A mentor suggested that I apply for the Autism CRC's Future Leaders Program. I was successful in my application and began my journey to self-discovery and repairing my self-esteem, self-confidence, and belief in my ability that was damaged by the negative leadership experience.

Future Leaders Program

The Autism CRC Future Leaders Program is 'Australia's first holistic leadership capacity building program for autistic adults. It was designed to empower autistic adults with leadership potential who want to make a positive impact in their communities' (Autism CRC, 2020a). The program is co-designed with autistic individuals for autistic individuals, with 80% of the project team and program facilitators being on the autism spectrum.

The program involves online modules, a three-day residential workshop, and a volunteer placement. During the online modules, I learned about my autism identity, self-advocacy, and various leadership styles which I used to develop my own leadership style using my autistic traits as strengths. I walked into the residential workshop, filled with self-doubt, wondering if I deserved to be in the program. However, it was the most supportive environment I had ever been in, one in which we could be our authentic self, no masking, no need to pretend to be something we are not. I felt totally accepted as an autistic person. We worked with experienced autistic advocates and leaders, we set our leadership goals, participated in group problem solving sessions, conducted presentations, participated in media training, and we were paired with a mentor who was also autistic and had a leadership role.

The benefits of my participation in Future Leaders was rebuilding belief in myself, that I am capable of being in leadership and developing my autistic pride. Prior to Future Leaders I didn't know other autistic adults like me and in my experiences at school as a student and teaching in schools, people looked down on those who have disabilities believing they can't be successful because of their disability, constantly saying they can't do something because of the label of a disability sitting above their head. After the residential workshops I had a newfound confidence, I was equipped with the skills and knowledge to successfully enter the world of leadership, and I was inspired by the things myself and my fellow Future Leaders Alumni had achieved on our journey.

> Autistic space or autism-friendly space considers how the physical space at school can be created to be more welcoming and support sensory needs.

Following the Future Leaders Program, I applied the knowledge and skills into my life in education. I changed my mindset from deficits-based to strengths-based approaches with my students' learning. I implemented elements of Autistic Space into my classrooms by allowing students to use fidget devices, listen to music, and if they wanted to sit on the floor on a beanbag or gym ball they could. Autistic space or autism-friendly space considers how the physical space at school can be created to be more welcoming and support sensory needs. After going over the rules about how to use fidgets as tools not toys, and how they can help us to concentrate, the students were allowed to use them in class. I was teaching in mainstream classes at the time with a handful of students in my classes having verified disabilities. To not make them stand out as different, all students in my classes were permitted to use the same strategies. This led to increased engagement in learning, a reduction in negative behaviours resulting in zero students being sent out of my classes for disruptive behaviour, and improvements in academic grades for all of my students. Feeling confident in teaching again and in my abilities, I applied for a leadership position at the end of the 2019 school year and was subsequently appointed as the Senior Inclusion Coordinator in the Special Education Program for the 2020 school year.

During Future Leaders, one of the big take-home messages for me was if you want to best meet the needs of the autistic community you need to ask them what they want or need. As the Case Manager of a number of autistic students I spend time speaking with each individual and observing them in their classrooms so I can help them to identify potential triggers or barriers to their learning. A number of them are not self-aware of their autistic traits or sensory triggers. I help them to understand how they process the environment around them and work with them to identify strategies that work for them. I often draw from my lived experience as examples of how they too can overcome their struggles to be successful and role model the strategies I use to help me navigate the world not built for us.

I identified through my own lived experience that a number of autistic students displayed behaviour in response to sensory issues or difficulties with changes in their routine. School staff had little understanding of these challenges and therefore responded in ways that reflected their lack of knowledge about autism. I've seen a range of intervention programs implemented with limited success. From what I understand, these programs were written or created by individuals not on the autism spectrum who do not have an intimate understanding of how an autistic brain works and understands the world around them. I decided to write a program myself drawing from my lived experience as a misunderstood autistic student and an educator with 10+ years teaching students on the autism spectrum. I facilitated a weekly session with eight students on the autism spectrum. In the very first session, we spoke about autism identity and all of them said they did not like the term Autistic Spectrum Disorder (ASD) and this is the common term used in the education setting. The students would prefer to be identified as autistic or on the autism spectrum. As a group we spoke about how we all disliked being called ASD because the D stands for disorder which to us implies we are broken or have something wrong. As the program went on, we discussed coping mechanisms and strategies which the students were then able to use in class. The implementation of these strategies resulted in a reduction in negative behaviour referrals, increase in engagement in class, and an improvement in academic grades.

Listening to the voices of people on the spectrum

In my experience, students with autism are rarely, if ever, consulted about their needs and what supports should be implemented. There is often engagement with parents or carers, classroom teachers, and case managers to determine support strategies and interventions for the student. But the person who the supports and interventions are implemented to assist more often than not do not have a voice.

As a student myself I had a challenging time in high school. I was seen as a naughty, disruptive student. I was often issued consequences like detentions and even put on behaviour monitoring programs because of my behaviour in class. I would fidget, draw, and wiggle around in my seat because I struggled to focus and concentrate. Almost all of my teachers didn't ever ask me what was going on in my world, what they could do to help me learn, how could they make adjustments to help support me in the classroom. They just focused on the negatives of what I couldn't do, things like 'why can't you just sit still', 'stop doodling', 'I need you to pay attention to me', 'look me in the eyes when I'm talking to you'. They constantly told me I was not good academically; they told me that I wouldn't be successful when I finished school. Thankfully for me when I hit Grade 9 there was a new teacher to the school who took me under her wing. Instead of constantly telling me how bad I was at school, she actually spent time with me in class and ensured that the curriculum was adjusted to support my learning. She let me fidget and move about, she never forced me to look her in the eyes. Instead of making me stay in at breaks for detentions, at breaks she would spend time with me to help me try to understand the challenges I was going through and plan how I could navigate school in a way I understood so I could be successful.

The first author of this chapter has created two infographics based on her lived experiences to help explain how an autistic person's brain processes and responds to the environment around them (see Figures 4.1 and 4.2).

The next section will focus on the first author's support for *inclusionED*[1] and describes how she will use this platform to support the inclusion of students on the autism spectrum.

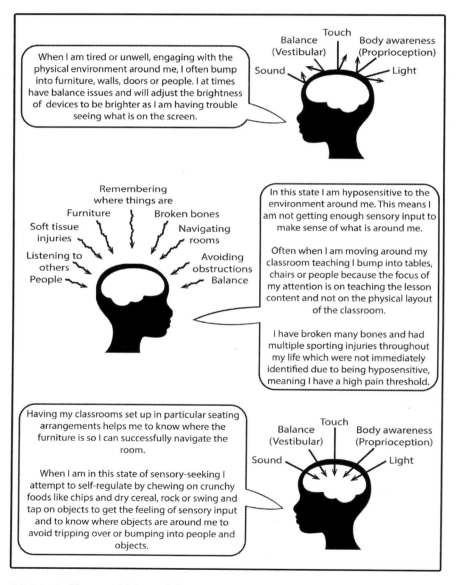

FIGURE 4.1 Hyposensitivity and the autistic brain.

Autistic voices in autism education research **57**

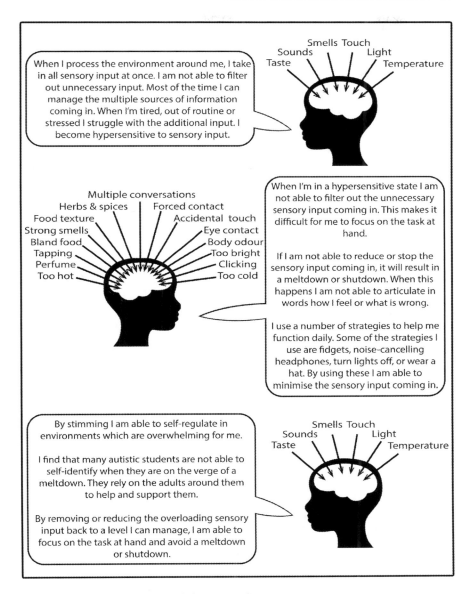

FIGURE 4.2 Hypersensitivity and the autistic brain.

As introduced in Chapter 3, *inclusionED* is an online platform that assists educators and parents to support students, whether they are at school or at home. The *inclusionED* practices and resources are underpinned by the outputs of over 25 research and development projects carried out through Autism CRC's School Years Program over the past six years involving many researchers and organisations. The platform is co-designed with educators, for educators, and provides evidence-based and research-informed teaching practices, videos, printable templates, and other resources designed to support diverse learners in inclusive classrooms. The platform also facilitates a national community of practice, enabling social sharing and educator reviews on the experience of implementing specific teaching practices.

My involvement in *inclusionED*

I am passionate about making school environments a better place for autistic students and ultimately more inclusive for everyone. This is why I became involved in inclusionED by being in the Research Advisory Group providing written feedback to the research team and beta testing of the website. Having the lived experience I did during my schooling years and seeing many autistic students struggling throughout my career, I wanted to be part of making schools more autistic-friendly a reality.

In my teaching experiences I have seen a number of students picked on for being neurologically different. Some of those students do not have the social skills understanding to realise they are being made fun of. I have witnessed mainstream students using the term SEP (Special Education Program) as an insult directed to students with disabilities and even on occasions flippantly directed to students who don't have a disability just to insult them. I use it as an educational experience for the students by saying, 'I'm extremely offended at how they have used the term in a derogatory way. I am technically SEP because I have autism and ADHD and you would never say anything like that to me'. With wide eyes and pale faces, the students quickly apologise to me and the other student.

My hope is that the roll out of inclusionED will upskill and empower teachers all over Australia to create inclusive classrooms for autistic students and students not on the spectrum. The database of resources on inclusionED's website is constantly being updated with evidence-based resources fully accessible for members to view, download, and use. It is free to use and my mainstream colleagues who have already started using the website have identified how useful the resources are and how readily they can access the content.

There was an autistic student who was having numerous behaviour issues in their Special Education modified class. Science is one of their interests so they were bored with the simplified content. This resulted in arguments with peers who called them a know-it-all. I suggested they come into my science class which was the same year level. They were quite capable academically but during their primary school years there had been negative social experiences for them with a number of the students in my class. So before they were moved into my class fulltime I spent a lesson educating the class about autism. The students knew I was autistic and ADHD and everyone had access to supports like fidgets or music. I showed the class a video of me being interviewed about being autistic from my media training during the Future Leaders Program, we had a class discussion as they genuinely wanted to learn more to better understand autism. By educating the class and putting strategies in place prior to the student moving into the class, this helped the student to successfully transition as well as ensured those who had negative experiences in the past feel like they were also supported. This made everyone feel respected and valued in the class. This student went from A's at Grade 4 level to comfortably passing Grade 8 Science with a C+ in one semester.

I have facilitated a Professional Learning Community (PLC) with a number of my colleagues called 'Removing Learner Barriers for Students on the Autism Spectrum'. In that PLC we have looked at what autism is, we have spoken about evidenced-based approaches to supporting autistic students and making classrooms more autistic friendly. A main part of this PLC has been looking at the inclusionED website, unpacking the resources on the website and then putting those strategies into practice with the autistic student who staff have chosen as a case study. A number of staff in the group excitedly registered and began looking through the website after our first meeting. During our collegial conversation they shared what they had trialled that worked and, more importantly, all of the participants identified that the strategies they implemented were not only successful with their autistic students but they found they were successful for all *students in their classes.*

> **TEACHER FEEDBACK ABOUT *inclusionED*:**
>
> I also would like to thank you for introducing me to this amazing website inclusionED which is highly informative and helpful. It not only caters to the needs of students with autism, but also provides strategies which can be useful for our diverse learners within the classrooms. I look forward to applying these techniques and the other strategies discussed with you to my pedagogy, and support my students in not only attaining their learning goals at school, but also help them prepare for life beyond school.

My perspectives of education research
What will make a difference?

Creating inclusive educational settings allows those of us on the autism spectrum to be included in mainstream classes instead of being withdrawn because of sensory or social differences. We don't need expensive refurbished rooms or costly educational resources. More often than not all we require is simply some empathy and understanding that we process the world around us and learn differently. The supports we use may seem unfair to peers like being able to wear a hat inside the room or having noise-cancelling headphones because they may not be allowed to wear a hat or have headphones but for autistic people those supports make it easier for us to concentrate and learn. This is why I allow all my students access to fidgets, music/headphones, to wear hats inside, or sit on an alternate seat because if everyone has access then no one stands out as different.

If the premise of autism education research is to support autistic students, then you must *include the voice of autistic students as well as their parents, teachers, and specialists. There is no blanket one-size-fits-all strategy and the only ones who can provide you with the valuable information you seek are autistic students.*

I have been the Queensland Athletes With Disabilities (AWD) Futsal Team Coach since 2015. Each year when we travel to National Titles, we travel with the mainstream Football Queensland Futsal Teams. We stay at the same hotel, have access to the same physios, and eat with the rest of the Queensland contingent like one big family. A number of the junior teams come to our venue to watch our games and excitedly ask how our games were when we arrive back at the hotel. I remember walking out for our first grand final at nationals seeing a sea of maroon in the stands supporting us. One year I had a conversation with the Tour Manager, and we spoke about how having the AWD team travel and stay with the juniors has helped develop a culture of inclusion and educated the younger players about how people with disabilities can also be successful when barriers are removed. I've had parents of the junior players comment about how their child's vision of people with disabilities has changed for the better as a result of their time around us. Older youth players have mentioned they don't see the AWD players as people with disabilities, they see them as Futsal players just like them. This supportive and inclusive Queensland team culture allows the AWD players to feel like they belong, giving them the confidence to perform at their best. This is what I hope becomes the cultural norm in schools in years to come. I hope that students with disabilities aren't labelled by their disability but are simply known as students just like their peers.

To build awareness and a culture of accepting differences I openly disclose my autism and ADHD diagnosis so students can see successful autistic adults showing them that people with disabilities can achieve their goals. I hope to inspire them to believe they too can achieve their aspirations. Part of that includes role modelling how to manage sensory needs in the classroom using strategies to focus and concentrate in class.

When I have asked autistic students for their feedback and discuss with them their individual autistic traits to identify what we can do to help support them, they smile and excitedly disclose, 'for once someone is actually asking me what will help me instead of another adult telling me what to do, when they don't understand how my brain works'. Another has disclosed, 'You are the first adult I have heard talk about my autism in a positive way, everyone else talks about it in a negative way as if I'm broken and need fixing'.

How Autism CRC's research and inclusionED can make a difference to education practice

Historically, for people gaining qualifications in special education, it has been taught that autism is a tragedy that needs to be treated with interventions and behaviour modification therapies. This has created a culture of only seeing autistic students by what they can't do and developing goals to address these perceived deficits. For myself as a student and early in my career, classrooms were conducted based on school policies and behaviour expectations that were one-size-fits-all and didn't consider disability-specific sensory needs. The expected norm was that everyone sits in their seat, quietly working, and those who did not were issued consequences or put into behaviour modification interventions. Basically, we were being conditioned to be less autistic and act more like our peers. As I developed my own teaching practice, I moved away from the traditional classroom model to a more sensory-friendly and inclusive one. I reflected on my schooling years and what didn't work for me and decided I didn't need to change my students. I wanted to make my classroom a place where students want to be, not lessons full of frustration and angst for them.

The research being conducted by the Autism CRC promotes the inclusion of autistic voice at all levels, is being used to create inclusive policies, promotes strengths-based approaches to learning, promotes respectful language and positive autistic identity, and creates positive change in the way in which those working with autistic individuals engage with and support them. It has been a long journey over a number of years, with still a way to go but I am seeing a change in the right direction. Particularly in my school where I am supported by my administration who allow me to use the strategies that I do every day, they support my engagement with the Autism CRC, allowing me time to collaborate with Autism CRC. They have had me present to the school population about neurodiversity and autism as well as seeking advice when dealing with or engaging autistic students and upskilling mainstream staff on working with autistic students.

Key messages to education researchers

1. *Nothing about us without us.* If your research is about autistic students make sure you have autistic voices involved at all levels, not just as participants. Those autistic voices can include parents of autistic students, teachers of autistic students, autistic researchers, but most importantly **must** include actual autistic students and adults, depending on your target audience.
2. *Language matters to us, even as children.* Historically, many people working in autistic support roles have been influenced by the medical model of thinking about people with disabilities discussed in Chapter 1 and use person-first language; for example, person with autism or student with autism. However, in my experience, most of the autistic community subscribe to the social model of disabilities (as discussed in Chapter 1) and would use identity-first language; for example, 'I am a proud autistic woman'. Please be respectful of how we identify and if you are unsure what to use, just ask us.
3. *Many of us don't like change and struggle with new people, particularly young people.* If you want to get the best outcomes for your research, meet us in an environment where we can perform our best, allow a support person to be present, and we will be more likely to engage.
4. *The method or methods in which you conduct your research need to be varied to meet the needs of your participants.* One method of communication may work for a number of people in our community but not all. If you want a true representation of our whole community, you can't just rely on a paper survey or online survey, just the same as you can't just rely on someone speaking over the phone. There needs to be a range of ways in which a participant can engage in the process.
5. *We want to be included just like everyone else in the same classrooms.* Research should be supporting the move towards inclusion and inclusive classrooms. This is what the autistic community wants for education.
6. *Autism education research should not just be about what can be done for the autistic students to make their schooling experiences better; there needs to be a vision of the bigger picture of full inclusion.* Consider how your research can be used to benefit the whole school community. We want to be able to be in mainstream classes like our peers and our peers want to be able to have access to the universal strategies that we use to help us.

Key messages to teachers and school leaders about their engagement in education research and their journey to inclusion

1. *Nothing about us without us.* If you are working with autistic students and want to know what will help them, ask them! Their parents or Case Managers will also have an understanding of what works for them, but classroom environments are dynamic; even the most

structured of classrooms can quite quickly become unstructured and lead to a meltdown or shutdown. There is almost always a catalyst to a behaviour episode; for example, a little spike in noise level could be a trigger. The only way to know what led to the episode is to remove the overloading issue then allow the student time to regulate themselves and then you can ask them what led to the situation to plan what can be done in future.

2. We are not all Rainman, nor do we all respond to the same strategies and interventions. It is not a one-size-fits-all community. You may have taught an autistic student or a number of autistic students and what worked for them was great but that doesn't mean everyone will respond in the same way. I like to use Rubik's cubes; for others it makes them frustrated. I hate the sensory feeling of putty and won't touch it but for many autistic people, they love it. Same with how you engage us in learning: we are all different. Some of us are creative, others of us are not imaginative, we are more logical and methodical.

3. Use our interests! If you are finding your autistic students are not engaging in the curriculum or struggling to understand the content, link it to our interests and you will find our engagement increases as we see value in doing it. If we don't see the point in it, we don't want to do it and see it as a waste of our time.

4. Use a strengths-based approach to our education. We already know we are different and there are a number of things we can't do that our peers can do; you don't need to constantly remind us of this fact. You can, however, focus on our strengths and how you can use them to help us to learn and be successful in the classroom.

5. Language matters to us, even as children. Most people are taught the medical model of disabilities where you identify people using person-first language; for example, student with autism. However, most of the autistic community subscribes to the social model of disabilities where we use identity-first language; for example, 'I am a proud autistic woman'. Please be respectful of how we identify and if you are unsure what to use, just ask us.

6. Autism education research should not just be about what can be done for the autistic students to make their schooling experiences better; there needs to be a vision of the bigger picture of full inclusion. Consider how the research can be used to benefit the whole school community. We want to be able to be in mainstream classes like our peers and our peers want to be able to have access to the universal strategies that we use to help us.

Transformation of research to support impact on the lives of autistic people

Inclusive education is about all of us and emphasises that none of us should be excluded (Cologon, 2019). Our approach in our research has been to ensure that the voices of the autistic community are not only heard along with educators and specialists who need to work together to support inclusion, but that education research needs to be informed, co-produced, and co-disseminated with autistic people. There are many inclusive ways of conducting research such as the approaches described in

> Our approach in our research has been to ensure that the voices of the autistic community are not only heard along with educators and specialists who need to work together to support inclusion, but that education research needs to be informed, co-produced, and co-disseminated with autistic people.

this chapter: i) participatory research; ii) voice research; and iii) co-production research. This chapter extends the range of descriptions of inclusive ways of conducting research by sharing real experiences that will inform future research planning for education researchers. The practical ideas that we provide to support researchers working in autism education research complements the suggestions in Chapter 2 about engaging with autistic individuals and their families. It has been acknowledged that education can play an important role in society by establishing models of working and respectful relationships to support an inclusive society (Hehir et al., 2016) and we would like to extend this idea by saying *transformational education research that values autistic voices* can play an important role in establishing inclusive schools.

Researcher reflections and future recommendations

Trudy Bartlett: *My involvement with Suzanne on inclusionED laid the foundations for us to work together on this book chapter. Initially I was surprised that Suzanne asked me to co-author on the chapter as I am still relatively new in the Autism Advocacy space and was not sure if I would be able to produce what Suzanne was looking for. Whilst I didn't think that I had the reputation or clout that warranted my words being put on the pages, Suzanne made it abundantly clear that she believed I was the right person to be co-authoring with her. She mentioned the radio interview that we did together about inclusionED and spoke about how my lived experiences were so valuable. She was confident that I would be able to complete the task she was asking of me. During our initial meeting she made it clear to me that she would support me in any way she needed to. Be it by email, face-to-face meeting or online meetings she would make time to meet with me when I needed. Initially I was extremely nervous about writing as it is not a strength of mine; however, together Suzanne and I created a clear plan which I was able to follow. Without a clear plan or direction I struggle to initiate tasks and often avoid them. I was extremely nervous when I submitted the first half of my draft, I expected to receive negative feedback and lots of notes indicating edits to be made, much like everything I ever wrote in English classes at school. However, Suzanne's response was not negative at all; it was quite the opposite, she loved what I wrote, and that filled me with pride and the confidence to complete the second half of my draft. I feel extremely honoured that I have been asked to contribute on this chapter and hope that my contributions help to make positive changes in the education system for autistic students and teachers.*

Suzanne Carrington: *I really wanted to co-author this chapter with an autistic person who could share their lived experience and provide practical ideas for improving research in education. I had met Trudy a couple of times at Autism CRC events and knew that she was a teacher and had been involved in the Future Leaders Program. We both had the opportunity to be interviewed together on the radio when inclusionED was launched. Trudy was truly the star and was very confident talking about what education research should be focusing on in order to have maximum impact for young people on the spectrum. I knew that she had a great story to share and I have enjoyed the collaborative writing process. I think this chapter and Trudy's contribution in particular will support future education research and educators who read this research to progress the development of inclusive education and move away from segregated and withdrawal programs in schools.*

Note

1 www.inclusioned.edu.au

References

Autism CRC. (2016). *Inclusive research practice guides and checklists for autism research: Version 2.* Brisbane: Cooperative Research Centre for Living with Autism (Autism CRC).
Autism CRC. (2020a). *Future Leaders 2018 evaluation report.* Brisbane: Cooperative Research Centre for Living with Autism (Autism CRC). Retrieved from https://www.autismcrc.com.au/knowledge-centre/reports/future-leaders-2018-evaluation-report.
Autism CRC. (2020b). *Participatory and inclusive autism research practice guides (Version 3).* Brisbane: Cooperative Research Centre for Living with Autism (Autism CRC).
Autism CRC. (2020c). *What is co-production?* Brisbane: Autism CRC. Retrieved from https://www.autismcrc.com.au/coproduction/what-is.
Cargo, M., & Mercer, S. L. (2008). The value and challenges of participatory research: Strengthening its practice. *Annual Review of Public Health*, 29(1), 325–350.
Carrington, S. (1999). Inclusion needs a different school culture. *International Journal of Inclusive Education*, 3(3), 257–268. doi:10.1080/136031199285039.
Carrington, S., Bland, D., & Brady, K. (2010). Training young people as researchers to investigate engagement and disengagement in the middle years. *International Journal of Inclusive Education*, 14(5), 449–462.
Carrington, S., & Holm, K. (2005). Students direct inclusive school development in an Australian secondary school: An example of student empowerment. *Australasian Journal of Special Education*, 29(2), 155–171.
Carrington, S., & Robinson, R. (2006). Inclusive school community: Why is it so complex? *International Journal of Inclusive Education*, 10(4–5), 323–334.
Cologon, K. (2019). *Towards inclusive education: A necessary process of transformation.* Melbourne: Children and Young People with Disability Australia.
Hehir, T., Grindal, T., Freeman, B., Lamoreau, R., Borquaye, Y., & Burke, S. (2016). *A summary of the evidence on inclusive education.* São Paulo: Alana Institute.
Israel, B. A., Schulz, A., Parker, E., Becker, A., Allen, A. I., & Guzman, J. (2003). Critical issues in developing and following community based participatory research principles. In M. Minkler & N. Wallerstein (Eds.), *Community based participatory research for health* (pp. 53–76). San Fransisco, CA: Jossey-Bass.
Long, J., Panese, J., Ferguson, J., Hamill, M. A., & Miller, J. (2017). Enabling voice and participation in autism services: Using practitioner research to develop inclusive practice. *Good Autism Practice*, 18(2), 6–14.
Nicolaidis, C., Raymaker, D., Kapp, S. K., Baggs, A., Ashkenazy, E., McDonal, K., ... Joyce, A. (2019). The AASPIRE practice-based guidelines for the inclusion of autistic adults in research as co-researchers and study participants. *Autism*, 23(8). doi:10.1177/1362361319830523
Pellicano, L., Mandy, W., Bölte, S., Stahmer, A., Lounds Taylor, J., & Mandell, D. S. (2018). A new era for autism research, and for our journal. *Autism*, 22(2), 82–83.
Raymaker, D., & Nicolaidis, C. (2013). Participatory research with autistic communities: Shifting the system. In J. Davidson & M. Orsini (Eds.), *Worlds of autism: Across the spectrum of neurological difference* (pp. 169–188). Minneapolis, MN: University of Minnesota Press.
Rudduck, J., & Flutter, J. (2004). *How to improve your school: Giving pupils a voice.* London: Bloomsbury Publishing.
United Nations. (1989). *Convention on the rights of the child.* Geneva: United Nations.

Walmsley, J., & Johnson, K. (2003). *Inclusive research with people with learning disabilities: Past, present and future*. London: Jessica Kingsley Publishers.
Watson, K. (2018). Unspeakable: The discursive production of a 'tragic subject' among children in the early childhood classroom. *International Journal of Inclusive Education*. doi:10.1 080/13603116.2018.1532535.

PART 3
Knowledge translation and research impact

Cogs Will Turn Just Differently (by Imogen, aged 12 years)

'This painting shows that the autistic mind may work differently but is still brave, trustworthy and amazing.'

5

WITH TEACHERS, FOR TEACHERS

Knowledge translation and professional learning

Michael Whelan, Jeremy Kerr, Keely Harper-Hill and Oksana Zelenko

> Previous chapters have focused on the importance of an inclusive approach to research that values equal partnerships with people on the autism spectrum. In this chapter, we explain how we collaborated with participants who were critically important to the knowledge translation process: classroom teachers and school staff. One of the benchmarks of successful research translation is to have a genuine impact on the everyday lives of 'end-users' and, in our case, this meant changing the practice of education professionals. This was an ambitious objective as changing school-based practices requires teacher agency, autonomy, and engagement. This chapter describes the co-design and consultation process with teachers to develop an online platform that addressed the real-life professional learning needs of Australian teachers. This chapter details the journey across the design and build phases of the online platform. It offers researchers who are committed to knowledge translation into classroom practices an array of insights into a process undertaken to optimise uptake of research by teachers and schools to benefit all students in Australian classrooms.

Between 2016 and 2020, the research team has undertaken a research program with a clearly defined brief:

- Initiate a national conversation with teachers to identify their professional learning needs and preferences to support them in meeting the needs of diverse learners in their classrooms.
- Design and build an elearning portal that reflects these expressed needs.

- Design a knowledge translation process that captures the diverse range of evidence-based research outcomes produced from the Autism CRC's School Years Program.
- Communicate these education research outcomes to Australian classroom teachers in a way that enables them to apply them in their everyday teaching practice.

The research team responded to the Autism CRC's call out for knowledge translation submissions in 2015, but instead of a stand-alone content project, the team proposed a whole-of-program solution to accommodate the 30-plus research projects in the Schools Years Program. The project commenced with a working title of 'Living Portal', an acknowledgement of the need for an active community of participants to implement content and share practitioner experiences among peers in the online community. The second working title was 'The Diverse Learners Hub', a more descriptive label that provided insight into the site's practice domain. In 2019, after consultation with multiple partners, and most importantly the Autism CRC's knowledge translation team, the new site was launched in May, 2020 as inclusionED.edu.au.

The *inclusionED* project was established to meet the collective needs of multiple stakeholders, including teachers, school principals, researchers, parents of students on the spectrum, and most importantly, young people on the autism spectrum. When viewed in isolation, the needs of each stakeholder group present a unique and complex range of professional, philosophical, and personal challenges. Teachers are time-poor and need professional learning opportunities and resources that meet their immediate learning and teaching needs. Researchers in education and allied health disciplines need to enact ethical and inclusive research programs which fulfil their project aims and then communicate their findings through the specialist discourses of peer-refereed academic journals. Parents of students on the autism spectrum are universally exhausted and often struggle to keep track of classroom activities and provide home support to support their child's learning development. Students on the autism spectrum need teachers who are well-trained, intuitive, and resourceful with ready access to best practice teaching and learning resources to meet their diverse learning needs.

> *The inclusionED project was established to meet the collective needs of multiple stakeholders, including teachers, school principals, researchers, parents of students on the spectrum, and most importantly, young people on the autism spectrum.*

When viewed as a collection, the multiple stakeholder needs listed above reveal a diverse range of professional, cultural, pedagogical, and technical cultures that rarely communicate in one coherent voice. The role of knowledge translation in the *inclusionED* project is of critical importance in an environment where these multiple voices require an architectural conduit to maintain both fidelity of message and flexibility of delivery. When the *inclusionED* project commenced in 2016, the Autism CRC had already produced a catalogue of completed research projects, some already published in national and international journals. With this growing library of research already established and with end-user uptake of evidence-based practices a key project aim, we commenced the process of engaging Australian teachers.

Professional learning and teaching practice

Professional learning opportunities for classroom teachers have a chequered legacy in transforming teaching practice. Factors that influence changes to teacher practice that occur in response to professional learning are dynamic and complex (Harper-Hill et al., 2020) and evidence suggests that many one-off professional development opportunities do not result in sustainable changes to classroom practice (Darling-Hammond & Richardson, 2009; Yoon, Duncan, Lee, Scarloss, & Shapley, 2007). The current research project focused specifically upon professional learning which would provide opportunities for teachers to transform their practice. Therefore, the term 'professional learning opportunities' has been adopted to describe experiences and activities undertaken by teachers which have the potential to lead to changes in teacher practice.

Educators who participated in the Autism CRC *Australian Autism Educational Needs Analysis* (ASD–ENA) (Saggers et al., 2018) identified that the current provision of suitable autism-specific education and training for educators and specialists was one of the top three barriers to their own professional learning. It is well established that teacher professional learning programs are uneven in their impact when measured by developing and transforming teacher classroom practice.

In comparison with their counterparts in OECD countries, Australian teachers were the least likely to describe any of the professional learning they received as having a moderate or high impact on their teaching (Freeman, O'Malley, & Eveleigh, 2014; OECD, 2013). It is important to interpret this information understanding its context. The data was collected from teachers of students in Years 7–9 and was in reference to general professional learning, not autism-specific professional learning. That these same teachers had identified their greatest professional learning was in the area of 'students with special needs' (NB: Not our language) is worth noting, particularly because less than a third had actually engaged in such professional learning activities.

Professional learning opportunities and online peer networks

Effective professional learning opportunities are those which address the learning needs of individual teachers (Louws, Meirink, van Veen, & van Driel, 2017; Visser, Evering, & Barrett, 2014), where these needs are determined by the teachers themselves and *endorse teacher judgement* as a factor in successful implementation of teacher practice (Dadds, 2014; Fiszer, 2004). Further, success is more likely if the professional learning opportunities are *school-based* (Cole, 2004). Incorporating peer-learning (Buczynski & Hansen, 2010), or potentially comprising a *networking community* (Kishida, 2011) including online peer-learning networks have been shown to effectively support teachers' professional learning (e.g., Visser et al., 2014), possibly because the combination of the activity and growing relationships among group members further promotes changes in teacher practice (Lock, 2006). Critical to the transfer of professional learning opportunities into practice are active applications of the targeted practice followed by reflection (Louws et al., 2017). Positioning *teachers as primary agents* in the identification of strengths and needs of professional learning within supportive reflective environments is therefore critical in the translation of this research into practice.

Findings from the research outlined above emphasise that optimising outcomes for teachers engaged in professional learning opportunities is complex and goes beyond direct teaching of technical practices to teachers. This conclusion echoes calls from the literature that teaching cannot be understood in the context of teachers as empty vessels (Rodriguez, 2012) nor as technicians who will invariably enact a solely 'technical process' with pre-determined outcomes independent of the needs of individual learners (Kemmis, 2014). The objective of this project was to design an elearning platform to support teachers' access to professional learning opportunities that would result in the adoption of evidence-based teaching practices in Australian schools and classrooms. Achieving this objective would be enhanced if the platform was co-designed to meet the specific needs of teachers as end-users of the platform.

Co-design as method of end-user engagement and research

The successful translation of new professional knowledge generated by the Autism CRC's School Years Program into educational practice was at the heart of the project's challenge. The aim of this platform was to facilitate teacher understanding and adoption of evidence-based practices, the success of which will ultimately be realised through improved student outcomes.

Co-design – or participatory design – is an established research methodology used to design or evaluate services or products with the people or community who use or are impacted by the service or product. Of particular relevance for this project was the premise that co-design acknowledges the expertise, values, and lived experience of the participants and can nurture a community of practitioners and ongoing participation.

> *The aim of this platform was to facilitate teacher understanding and adoption of evidence-based practices, the success of which will ultimately be realised through improved student outcomes.*

The challenges around establishing this community of practice were heightened in the Australian context where teachers are employed across government, Catholic, and independent education sectors. While individual state and territory governments are constitutionally responsible for the provision of education services to all school-age children in their jurisdiction, their primary fiscal responsibility is to state schools. In contrast, non-government sectors in the states and territories receive the majority of their funding through the Commonwealth Government of Australia (Australian Government, 2020). So, in order for the planned platform to have the capacity to accommodate the needs of various education sectors across Australian states and territories, its development would rely upon the involvement of both state and national participants, which became a touchstone of the project's design.

Co-design journey: From online workshops to group user testing

Socio-technical systems such as websites and learning portals that are designed in partnership with users are more likely to deliver models that will align directly with their needs and are more likely to succeed than those imposed by 'experts' (Lin, Hughes, Katica, Dining-Zuber, & Plsek, 2011; Orlowski et al., 2016; Zelenko, Gomez, & Kelly, 2021). In order to translate knowledge from the Autism CRC authentically and effectively, a participatory design process was developed and enacted. The co-design philosophy and democratic principles are also strongly aligned with the Autism CRC's educational philosophies of inclusion, reciprocity, and respect. In applying these principles across the *inclusionED* project, the research team collaborated with a wide range of stakeholders from across Australia with classroom teachers, specialist support teachers, policy makers, students on the spectrum, their parents, and also participants from partner specialist service provider organisations such as Positive Partnerships.

These design collaborations commenced with an open and frank acknowledgement that the co-design process can be messy at times and lack clarity, particularly relevant for practical professionals such as time-poor teachers who can be task oriented. Having acknowledged this 'fuzzy front-end' (Herstatt & Verworn, 2004) of the co-design journey, we commenced a design process that over four and a half years has led to the launch of the *inclusionED* website and learning community portal.[1] An additional and unique challenge facing the *inclusionED* team was the remote nature of the research and the implementation of a 'virtual co-design' process. While face-to-face engagement with co-design participants can be critical to a project's success, virtual co-design can be highly effective in a number of delivery scenarios (Näkki et al., 2011).

The *inclusionED* co-design approach was blended, using a combination of virtual and in-person participation as our preferred format, with small groups at the host location and individuals joining via video conferencing creating a sense of 'presence over distance'. Reilly et al. (2010) note that some physical and social cues may not translate in this mixed-media environment and we found instinctively that the facilitation style throughout the workshops projected an expressive, heightened, and performative quality in compensation for the distant participants.

Following, and in response to, the initial workshop phase of the research, an extended co-design framework was developed to guide the project implementation. These key stages of project creation were later branded as the:

1. Design stage.
2. Develop stage.
3. Implement stage.

Within each of these three stages a series of participatory practices and co-design activities were integrated and implemented.

Design stage

A pilot co-design workshop was undertaken to test and refine the overall toolkit design for the 'front end' co-design sessions. The pilot involved five teachers, all of whom were undertaking postgraduate studies in the area of special needs. The then research team produced an informal but informative short video to introduce us to workshop participants, which was emailed via a YouTube link. In addition to personal talking head introductions from each of the team, the video outlined project aims, estimated timelines, and proposed milestones in the project. The video style was generous, personal, and friendly in order to set the tone for our future non-hierarchical, collaborative workshops.

Workshops with stakeholders

In response to feedback from the workshop pilot, the combined virtual and in-person workshops were delivered to establish the themes, priorities, and design approaches that would lead to the development of a preliminary digital prototype. A total of 28 participants from around Australia in regional, remote, and metropolitan schools attended a series of nine workshops over a four-month period. Separate sessions were undertaken with the following cohorts:

FIGURE 5.1 Co-design workshop: Three online and two in-person.

With teachers, for teachers **75**

1. Classroom teachers and specialist support teachers.
2. Students with autism.
3. Parents of students with autism.
4. Education organisation policy makers and specialist service provider representatives.

The participants in the co-design workshops were recruited from Western Australia, Tasmania, New South Wales, and Queensland, from independent, Catholic, and government schools with policy maker participants from three national specialist organisations and one state-based organisation. This chapter focuses on the contribution of the key stakeholder group: teachers.

Individual workshops with teachers took place over two hours and entailed a series of design thinking-based activities that were developed to provoke reflection and creative play. This format allowed teachers to discuss and explore learning possibilities and barriers in a relaxed and spontaneous way. Following icebreaker activities, which allowed participants both in-person and online to become familiar with each other, an introductory visual mapping exercise was introduced (Figure 5.2). This activity required participants to reflect upon what they considered to have been their 'best learning experience', whereby they had learnt something new *and then used this within their classroom or school*. The teacher participants were guided through this activity by the facilitator, with examples of a range of different learning experiences, formal or informal. Participants were asked to consider learning experiences that could relate to an individual student, a small group of students, an entire class, across the whole school, or be related solely to other teachers and staff. Examples were given of how the learning experiences might encompass responding

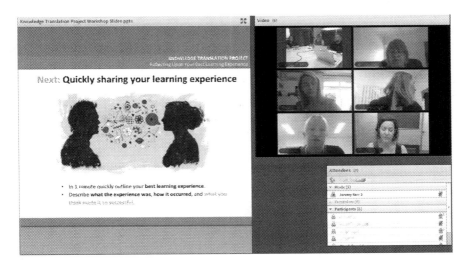

FIGURE 5.2 Design researcher Dr Jeremy Kerr facilitates an online co-design session: Five online and two in-person.

to a specific student need and then actively researching and implementing a solution. This was followed by talking with colleagues and hearing about a strategy and then applying it, finding an innovative teaching approach in professional learning and adapting it for use, or coming across an approach online or in a newspaper by chance and then investigating it further. Once explained, each teacher had 10 minutes to brainstorm five to 10 examples of their 'best learning experiences'. Upon doing this, they were then asked to circle the one they found most inspiring and found most exciting.

Having identified their top-ranking learning experience that led to teacher practice change, each teacher reflected on it from start to finish through drawing a visual map which captured 'the journey' of the experience. This visual map approach enabled reflections to be text-based and visual, which allowed for quick documentation of all steps and aspects. While teachers drew the maps, the facilitator provided further guidance of elements to consider and record on them, such as types of information sources utilised (visual and written, video, people, etc.) and what type of *learning communities* were accessed and established. Specific reference was also made for teachers to record any difficulties experienced at any step of the process, as well as the *emotional journey* they experienced. Teachers were also asked to document/include those *core values and themes* which were underlying the learning experience (such as empathy, guidance, peer connection, self-directed learning, etc.). All teachers then shared the map they had created and verbally described the experience to their fellow participants which was critical in the data collection process. Each presentation was recorded and the transcript analysed in conjunction with each teacher's map, ensuring all details and reflections were captured.

Following this reflective exercise, teachers were then given a creative challenge, wherein they were to apply their understanding of the learning experience that they had explored to how future learning opportunities could be designed. Teachers were asked to creatively imagine and visually map how their learning experience could be re-designed and improved for the year 2020 (three years in the future at the time). To support this task, teachers were presented with a series of 'megatrends', identified by the CSIRO as having major impact on Australia over the next 20 years. Included here was reference to individuals being more connected through digital technology (the 'virtually here' megatrend; Hajkowicz, Cook, & Littleboy, 2012). Again, prior to drawing a visual map of the learning experience, participants were encouraged to brainstorm and generate as many ideas as possible, before developing any that resonated with them most.

In re-designing their positive learning experiences, teachers were directed to think about which elements could be *enhanced by technology* and what could *not* be replaced by it, and to incorporate this into their work. They were also encouraged to be experimental in their approaches and to break established rules and conventions for learning if they felt inclined. Notably, the short-term future scenario meant the teachers could play with possibilities with technology, but not create models that reached the level of 'science fiction'. Designs were still firmly planted in the 'real world'. Teachers then shared their maps with others, highlighting what the experience was and what they had 'taken out' and what they had 'added' in this revised learning experience. Before finishing with the maps, all participants were then asked to circle in colour what elements of the design they thought would be essential or strongly desired in order to facilitate teacher practice change.

Building upon these individual designs and this final reflection, the final workshop activity required all participants to collaboratively design a group-based visual map for an ideal learning system for the year 2020. This was a learning system to directly support teachers to change current or adapt new practices. Through discussion, all participants contributed to the development of key elements of the system – its values, pedagogies, forms of media, types of interactions, etc. The facilitator documented all contributions on a group map, often asking participants to detail aspects further and validate what was being recorded. The map and workshop transcripts then, again, worked in conjunction to capture the full richness of ideas proposed.

Data analysis

The online and in-person workshops provided an opportunity for teachers to describe and design a professional learning model to meet their current and future needs. Following a process of visual and textual analysis of the design models, concept maps, and learning priorities provided by teachers during the co-design process, we were able to identify a set of four common themes or principles common to all cohorts whether they were primary, secondary, state school, or independent educators (Figure 5.3).

The core themes that emerged from the research were as follows: strong foundation; efficient discovery; supported implementation; and learning community.

1. Strong foundation: Our co-design participants described how educators needed to access easily digestible explanations of the evidence base within the context of current knowledge of autism in order to evaluate new teaching practices and understand the mechanisms by and conditions within which they

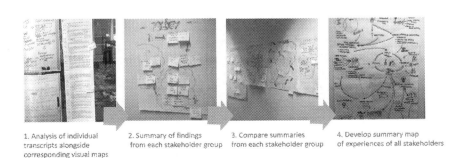

FIGURE 5.3 Stages in visual and thematic analysis.

were successful. Simply put, they needed to know that the classroom activity, or whole-of-school program, was based upon or informed by best practice research.
2. Efficient discovery: Our co-design participants described the obstacles finding professional learning resources that supported them in addressing specific challenges in the classroom. Entering a search engine term to locate a strategy or resource to support a teacher with a specific classroom challenge can yield up to 250,000 hits in a few seconds but will yield very little information on their efficacy and pedagogical rigour. Teachers want to be able to find the right professional learning resources for each specific situation as it arises with a minimum of clicks.
3. Supported implementation: Our co-design partners told us that in addition to the efficient discovery of quality teaching and learning supports, they wanted expert support in the implementation of these practices in the classroom. They wanted the narrative of implementation unpacked and delivered through video with experienced teachers demonstrating the practices in action using the resources provided; a practical guide to step them through the iterative process of planning, implementation, and reflection.
4. Learning community: Teachers in our co-design journey acknowledged the isolation that can be an obstacle to consolidating professional learning and the impact that the absence of sharing experiences of teaching practice can have. Teachers in smaller schools and in regional and remote areas were clear that to maximise the effectiveness of turning new knowledge into new practice in their classrooms, they need a supportive learning community and support to implement strategies. Teachers wanted to learn with others and to receive recognition for their time/effort in professional learning.

Combining findings from the textual and visual analysis with these four guiding themes or principles, a prototype website was created (see Figures 5.4 and 5.5 for examples of this). In addition to responding to the co-design findings, the prototype was also informed by advice from state-based education department technology infrastructure staff, interactive design literature, and the creative visual instincts of the designers on the research team. One of the visual metaphors that emerged on numerous occasions during the co-design process when discussing the concept of a learning community was that of social media. The practice of liking, sharing, following, commenting, and posting was well established in social media and the idea of capitalising on this well-known online vocabulary was mentioned numerous times in discussion with participants and among the research team.

Another online tool visualisation was drawn from film streaming services such as Netflix where content is sometimes categorised as 'New Release', 'Trending Now', 'if you liked "x" content then you might like "y" content', and film is categorised into genres such as 'Drama', 'Action', 'Romance', and 'Thriller'. These were translated into categories such as 'Classroom Management', 'Sensory Considerations', 'Home School Communications', and 'Transition Planning', into which a series of

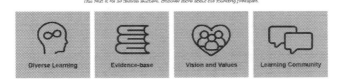

FIGURE 5.4 Prototype homepage: Provisional title: *Diverse Learners Hub*.

evidence-based teaching practices could be effectively themed including a five-star rating system for user evaluation.

Combining the visual metaphors and established practices from widely used popular culture interfaces with current literature in interactive visual design were the key ingredients in developing the prototype for what would be taken back to teachers for a process of concept validation.

Develop stage

Once the prototype was completed, the design was taken back to the co-design participants in the form of a user experience video where one of the research team previewed the user experience using screen capture and voice over. This video operated as a 'walk through' of a teacher using the platform, along with sharing the key themes that had emerged from all initial co-design workshops. After watching this video tour, participants completed an online survey consisting of closed- and open-ended questions, allowing for comprehensive feedback to be gathered. In collating the data, it became evident that respondents were extremely satisfied with the

FIGURE 5.5 Prototype: Practice categories.

platform and supported the overall design direction. In terms of critical feedback, the one area raised by some participants was adjusting some of interface options to allow easier navigation across the platform. Following validation of the prototype, a second, more detailed iteration was developed, which also incorporated the interface suggestions. This second prototype was then presented to other teachers, who had not been part of the research and design process, through a series of interactive showcases.

Two key presentations of the prototype occurred as scheduled events where teachers were the primary audience. This was firstly presented at the national 2018 Autism Spectrum Australia (Aspect) Autism in Education Conference and then the Brisbane Catholic Education (Springwood) Support Teacher Inclusive Education forum. In both cases, a live digital survey instrument, Mentimeter, was used for quantitative audience feedback via participants' mobile phones while the researchers presented multiple user journeys across the prototype. These surveys tested both the pedagogical integrity and design functionality of the prototype. At both events,

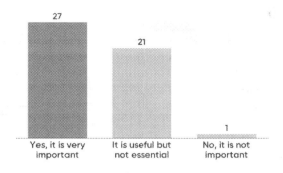

FIGURE 5.6 Real-time onscreen display of teacher response to a question. Brisbane Catholic Education (Springwood).

participants were asked 19 questions and the results were published immediately on screen for the audience, allowing for the group to discuss and reflect on findings (Figure 5.6). Semi-structured discussions then occurred with both groups at the end of each presentation with key points documented. At the Autism in Education Conference, approximately 30 educators and parents undertook the survey, while at Brisbane Catholic Education (Springwood) Support Teacher Inclusive Education forum, 80 participants took part.

The success of the prototype was indicated through consistent positive responses from participants across both events. Both teacher-based audiences indicated strong satisfaction in the design of the platform and saw it as a much-needed resource they expected to use often. In the discussion following the showcase, audience members also suggested wanting to see a further use of authentic classroom demonstrations across the platform and where possible the inclusion of student perspectives. These elements were then integrated at a further level into the final design of the platform.

Implement stage

Following the larger-scale teacher feedback and validation of the design, the formal build of the platform began. Significantly, integrated into this stage, was a further, ongoing co-design component with teachers, to assist with the further development of content and design elements. This collaboration occurred through the formal establishment of an advisory group for the platform. Members of this committee elected to be involved through responding to calls made on the Autism CRC Facebook page, via email to teachers on the Autism CRC newsletter lists, invitations to participants in prior co-design sessions, and through announcements at conference and presentation forums. Over 120 volunteer teachers and specialist educators responded to this initial call and became active participants in the committee. Participant involvement in the advisory group occurred – and continues to occur – asynchronously via email, with selected sub-groups of members being assigned evaluation and creative feedback tasks related to particular content and designs being developed for the platform. This continues to occur on an ongoing basis as research is further translated into content for the platform. Alongside collaboration with teachers via the Advisory Committee, on-site user testing also occurred with teachers as the build was occurring. This occurred in-person with a facilitator and using a *talk aloud* protocol. The *talk aloud* protocol involved individual teachers using the platform for a series of tasks and providing verbal feedback of their experience, highlighting what worked well and what they liked, as well as any problems and what they did not like. Specific questions were also canvassed ranging from language usage and features such as alignment to the AITSL (Australian Institute for Teaching and School Leadership) guidelines (AITSL, 2012).

Knowledge translation – Creating an authentic conduit

At the time of writing, the knowledge translation research and development process is ongoing with consideration focusing upon two central processes: text to rich media reimagining, and evidence-based verses evidence-informed teaching practices.

Unlike the standard research outputs of final report and academic journal publications, the final design iteration of *inclusionED* contains a range of information formats that reflect the co-design process. These content formats include text, image, infographic, video, animation, activity handouts, pedagogical approaches, process hierarchies, and implementation checklists. This diversity of media used in *inclusionED* is richer and more diverse than the more traditional research outputs which can privilege text and the occasional graph or diagram. The reimagining and subsequent transformation of research text into multimedia materials for the co-designed *inclusionED* format brings three disciplines into conversation:

- Research.
- Learning design.
- Education pedagogy.

This three-way interaction is emerging as a critical component in the knowledge translation process, not only in packaging of research content into practice content on *inclusionED* but in the way the funding body's research EOIs are framed, research methods employed, data collection approached, end-user and participant involvement, and quantifiable research outputs delivered. Recommendations regarding processes and guidelines for each of these stages will be a core output of the final knowledge translation research.

The second ongoing area of research and development in knowledge translation is articulating opportunities and frameworks to guide the development and publication of both evidence-based verses evidence-informed teaching practices. Some researchers may have already imagined how the outcomes of their research will translate to real-world applications for educators with specific classroom practices in mind from conception of the research. In other projects, the implications for end-user implementation of research may only materialise towards the closing stages of the projects.

Some research projects may support the development of a single classroom practice, while others may deliver a suite of related practices that can be implemented in classroom or whole-of-school settings. The challenge of this aspect of the knowledge translation process will be to distil with fidelity (where those components critical to fidelity are known) the rich research data into a format which reflects the express professional learning needs of classroom teachers. It is within this nexus that the spectrum of evidence-based and evidence-informed will be articulated in future publications.

At the time of publication, an iterative series of trials have been undertaken to develop a research translation toolkit that will support researchers in the quest to efficiently and effectively translate the findings from their research projects. The primary focus of these trials has been to scaffold researchers' efforts to translate findings according to the design and communication principles identified during the series of co-design activities and teacher consultations described above. The trials provided information that, while collected iteratively, has been used collectively to inform the current position knowledge translation process.

inclusionED – Live

The hallmark of the *inclusionED* research project has been its interdisciplinarity and participant goodwill through the navigation of multiple and discrete discourses, and through active participation of diverse stakeholder groups. And at its epicentre has been the continuing conversation with teachers. Continued collaboration with our end-users is a critical ingredient for research impact, not just for our project, but for the School Years Program of the Autism CRC.

> *Continued collaboration with our end-users is a critical ingredient for research impact, not just for our project, but for the School Years Program of the Autism CRC.*

The establishment of the *inclusionED* learning community is growing apace. Since its launch on May 18, 2020, *inclusionED* has had an immediate impact upon teachers across Australia with over 7,000 unique users and more than 1,200 registered members joining our exciting new learning community in the past six weeks alone. In addition to the rapid growth of learning community registrations, the reach of *inclusionED* is quite diverse with just over 30% of the learning community based in regional and remote schools outside of Australia's major cities. It's not just

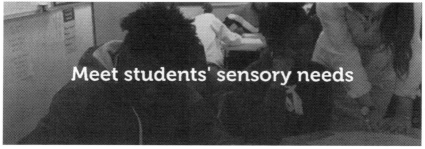

Resources are provided with this practice
Yes

Summary

Students on the autism spectrum often have specific sensory needs that, when unmet, can lead to inattentiveness, meltdowns, and inappropriate behaviour.

Making adjustments to accommodate these needs reduces the need for behaviour management and helps students to engage, attend, focus, and self-regulate during class. Adjustments can also significantly benefit all students by creating a more comfortable environment.

FIGURE 5.7 *inclusionED* – Teacher practice.
Source: www.inclusioned.edu.au.

Australian educators who are engaging with *inclusionED*, with just over 10% of visitors joining our community of practice from countries including New Zealand, the United States, the Philippines, and Singapore.

The role of this growing learning community will be critical for *inclusionED* to meet its true potential as a thriving educational research and practice ecosystem. The peer-to-peer learning and community building offered by the site's share, rate, and comment functionality has the potential not only to establish and nurture a community of practice but also to provide researchers with critical user feedback on the implementation of their school-based research. The joyful and productive dialogue established with classroom teachers around Australia has been the standout experience of the *inclusionED* research project. The willingness of teachers to share their values, experiences, and professional learning priorities suggests that future co-design ventures will yield positive outcomes for researchers, teachers, and, most of all, diverse learners.

How the practice works

Apply this practice with your students

The tabs below provide information to support your implementation of this practice. The sequence aligns with the Australian Institute for Teaching and School Leadership's High-Quality Professional Learning Cycle. You can find out more about high quality professional learning in the **Australian Charter for the Professional Learning of Teachers and School Leaders**.

| A. Plan |
| B. Set goals |
| C. Apply the practice |
| D. Reflect and refine |
| E. Share |

FIGURE 5.8 *inclusionED* – Implementation.
Source: www.inclusioned.edu.au.

Note

1 www.inclusioned.edu.au

References

Australian Government. (2020). *How are schools funded in Australia?* Canberra: The Department of Education, Skills and Employment. Retrieved from https://docs.education.gov.au/system/files/doc/other/how_are_schools_funded_in_australia_8.pdf.

Australian Institute for Teaching and School Leadership (AITSL). (2012). *Australian professional standards for teachers*. Retrieved from https://www.aitsl.edu.au/teach/standards

Buczynski, S., & Hansen, C. B. (2010). Impact of professional development on teacher practice: Uncovering connections. *Teaching and Teacher Education, 26*(3), 599–607.

Cole, P. (2004). *Professional development: A great way to avoid change.* Melbourne: Incorporated Association of Registered Teachers of Victoria (IARTV).
Dadds, M. (2014). Continuing professional development: Nurturing the expert within. *Professional Development in Education*, 40(1), 9–16.
Darling-Hammond, L., & Richardson, N. (2009). Research review/teacher learning: What matters? *Educational Leadership*, 66(5), 46–53.
Fiszer, E. P. (2004). *How teachers learn best: An ongoing professional development model.* Lanham, MD: ScarecrowEducation.
Freeman, C., O'Malley, K., & Eveleigh, F. (2014). *Australian teachers and the learning environment: An analysis of teacher response to TALIS 2013: Final Report.* Retrieved from https://research.acer.edu.au/talis/2.
Hajkowicz, S., Cook, H., & Littleboy, A. (2012). *Our future world: Global megatrends that will change the way we live. The 2012 revision.* Melbourne: CSIRO.
Harper-Hill, K., Beamish. W., Hay. S., Whelan. M., Kerr. J., Zelenko. O., & Villalba., C. (2020). Teacher engagement in professional learning: What makes the difference to teacher practice? *Studies in Continuing Education.* doi:10.1080/0158037X.2020.1781611.
Herstatt, C., & Verworn, B. (2004). The 'fuzzy front end' of innovation. In T. Durand, D. Probert, O. Granstrand, A. Nagel, A. B. Tomlin, C. Herstatt, & H. Tschirky (Eds.), *Bringing technology and innovation into the boardroom: Strategy, innovation and competences for business value* (pp. 347–372). New York, NY: Palgrave Macmillan. doi:10.1057/9780230512771_16.
Kemmis, S. (2014). Praxis, practice and practice architectures. In S. Kemmis, J. Wilkinson, C. Edwards-Groves, I. Hardy, P. Grootenboer, & L. Bristol (Eds), *Changing practices, changing education* (pp. 25–41). Singapore: Springer Singapore. doi:10.1007/978-981-4560-47-4.
Kishida, Y. (2011). Changes in teachers' practices following their participation in an autism-specific professional development program. *Special Education Perspectives*, 20(1), 29–39.
Lin, M., Hughes, B. L., Katica, M. K., Dining-Zuber, C., & Plsek, P. E. (2011). Service design and change of systems: Human-centered approaches to implementing and spreading service design. *International Journal of Design*, 5(2), 73–86.
Lock, J. V. (2006). A new image: Online communities to facilitate teacher professional development. *Journal of Technology and Teacher Education*, 14(4), 663–678.
Louws, M. L., Meirink, J. A., van Veen, K., & van Driel, J. H. (2017). Teachers' self-directed learning and teaching experience: What, how, and why teachers want to learn. *Teaching and Teacher Education*, 66, 171–183.
Näkki, P., Bäck, A., Ropponen, T., Kronqvist, J., Hintikka, K. A., Harju, A., … Kola, P. (2011). *Social media for citizen participation. Report on the Somus project.* Espoo: VTT Publications.
OECD. (2013). *Education policy outlook: Australia.* Retrieved from http://www.oecd.org/education/profiles.htm.
Orlowski, S., Matthews, B., Bidargaddi, N., Jones, G., Lawn, S., Venning, A., & Collin, P. (2016). Mental health technologies: Designing with consumers. *JMIR Human Factors*, 3(1), e4. doi:10.2196/humanfactors.4336.
Reilly, D., Voida, S., McKeon, M., Le Dantec, C., Bunde-Pedersen, J., Forslund, C., … Want, R. (2010). Space matters: Physical-digital and physical-virtual codesign in inSpace. *IEEE Pervasive Computing*, 9(3), 54–63. doi:10.1109/MPRV.2010.22.
Rodriguez, V. (2012). The teaching brain and the end of the empty vessel. *Mind, Brain, and Education*, 6(4), 177–185. doi:10.1111/j.1751-228X.2012.01155.x.
Saggers, B., Klug, D., Harper-Hill, K., Ashburner, J., Costley, D., Clark, T., … Carrington, S. (2018). *Australian autism educational needs analysis: What are the needs of schools, parents and students on the autism spectrum?* Brisbane: Cooperative Research Centre for Living with Autism (Autism CRC).

Visser, R. D., Evering, L. C., & Barrett, D. E. (2014). Twitter for teachers: The implications of Twitter as a self-directed professional development tool for K–12 teachers. *Journal of Research on Technology in Education*, 46(4), 396–413.

Yoon, K. S., Duncan, T., Lee, S. W. Y., Scarloss, B., & Shapley, K. (2007). *Reviewing the evidence on how teacher professional development affects student achievement* (Issues and Answers Report No. 033). Washington, DC: US Department of Education, Regional Educational Laboratory Southwest.

Zelenko, O., Gomez, R., & Kelly, N. (2021). Research co-design: A design-led framework to enable meaningful collaboration in research. In A. Blackler & E. Miller (Eds.), *How to be a design academic: From learning to leading*. Boca Raton, FL: CRC Press.

6

MEETING THE NEEDS OF ALL

The case to translate the evidence base beyond autism

Keely Harper-Hill, Michael Whelan and Beth Saggers

> In this chapter, the authors move from a concept of knowledge *translation* to *mobilisation* where teachers are deemed to be the agents through which research findings are enacted. By focusing on mobilisation into highly varied classroom contexts, the importance of including classroom teachers throughout the research process is highlighted. It is within this context of variable classroom settings that the story behind the whole-of-program knowledge mobilisation approach taken by the School Years Program is told. At the centre of the story is the challenge to respond to both the needs of teachers and researchers. In the *inclusionED* project described in Chapter 5, teachers called for findings to be translated in such a way that they could be used to meet the needs of a range of students in their class, not only those students on the autism spectrum. The *inclusionED* researchers were then required to explore the tension created between the needs of teachers as consumers and the needs of researchers as producers of research. The *inclusionED* project provides rich knowledge mobilisation experiences which will enhance the understandings of others entering into research collaborations. These experiences will also inform future considerations for whole-of-program approaches to knowledge mobilisation with the aim of optimising research impact.

We are committed to an inclusive approach to education that recognises and supports a diversity in learners. Through our collaborative research work with schools, teachers, parents, and students, we have come to understand that education is only inclusive if there is a shared commitment to the values and practice of inclusion. The aim of this chapter is to share our vision and research approach of meeting the needs of teachers *and* researchers to support inclusion and cater to the vast diversity they experience in students in 21st century classrooms.

Students in inclusive classrooms not only have a broad range of cultural, ethnic, religious, linguistic, and domestic backgrounds but also bring to the classroom a wide range of abilities and experiences (Green & Cherrington, 2010). This diversity makes the work of the contemporary teacher 'multidimensional and remarkably complex' (Good, 2008, p. 3). Teachers need to not only support the academic achievement of their students but also promote their personal, social, and moral development while also preparing them for their place in the everchanging, often unpredictable, and unstable landscape of the 21st century world (Good, 2008). One group of students who may present unique challenges to schools and are part of the growing diversity in mainstream classrooms are students on the autism spectrum (Saggers, Tones, Dunne, & Aberdein, 2019).

Research in the context of the inclusive classroom

The complexity of teachers' work in inclusive school settings is multifaceted. One layer of this complexity results from the diversity of needs, experiences, and ability of students. Additionally, school and classroom contexts are highly variable and add further layers to the complexity of teachers' work (Good, 2008). The implications of this are that when catering to the diversity of students, teachers' work is also shaped, influenced, and complicated by the context of their work:

> … individual teachers may interpret and respond to different contexts differently. Contexts may shape the structure of teachers' work (e.g., roles, tasks, and activities) and how teachers perform their work within that structure. Different contexts may be aligned and operate in a mutually reinforcing manner, or they may conflict.
>
> (Good, 2008, p. 8)

It is no wonder, therefore, that many contemporary teachers feel overwhelmed and under-supported, expressing concerns that they are inadequately prepared to meet the ever-increasing complexities of their role (Green & Stormont, 2018).

In order to address the multiple and often complex needs of their classrooms and students, teachers are under renewed and increasing pressure to ensure they are implementing practices that are informed by a range of instructional, social, and behavioural evidence-based practices (Markle & Lamont, 2013). Educators are being increasingly encouraged to use 'research evidence to inform their instructional practice', particularly in relation to meeting the needs of students on the spectrum (Marder & deBettencourt, 2015, p. 5). According to Marder and deBettencourt (2015, p. 6):

> … the use of EBPs [evidence-based practices] has been shown to improve student outcomes; however, they do not work with all students. It is critical

that educators understand how to select and implement a best practice with the students they are currently teaching.

While research can demonstrate the benefits of an intervention used in tightly controlled, ideal conditions (i.e., efficacy studies), further investigation on whether the same efficacious intervention is *effective* when used in the messy and unpredictable context of real-world practice (i.e., effectiveness studies) is necessary. While practices may have an evidence base, they may lack 'external' or social validity (Callahan et al., 2017), decreasing the likelihood that teachers will decide to adopt them in their particular education context and for their group of students.

According to Luiselli and Reed (2011, p. 1406), social validity refers to 'the acceptability of and satisfaction with intervention procedures, usually assessed by soliciting opinions from the people who receive and implement them'. Measures of social validity play a critical but under-utilised role in understanding the factors which lead educators to translate research knowledge to their practice and context. In a recent review investigating evidence-based practices and emerging treatments identified by the National Autism Center (NAC) and National Professional Development Center on Autism Spectrum Disorders (NPDC), Callahan et al. (2017) found that only a startling 26.7% of 828 articles cited direct measures of social validity. It is unclear how evidence-informed practices can be developed for inclusive classrooms without consistent evaluation of social validity within the classroom context. Given the role that teacher professional judgement plays in adopting teaching practices, this evaluation is critical as teachers decide whether a practice with an established evidence base will, in fact, be a good fit for their classroom.

In their 2017 research report into the evaluation of evidence-informed teaching in England, Coldwell and colleagues identified that teachers value research and that access to research findings was a necessary pre-requisite for evidence-informed teaching practice. However, in and of itself, access to these research findings was not sufficient. Evidence-informed teaching practice was more likely to be realised when teachers were able to trial application of findings to their own teaching practice informally or through more systematic action research. Importantly, this process of trial and error was characterised as being practice-driven with teachers being enabled to engage in practice reflection (Coldwell et al., 2017).

This is not to deny the merit of calls for teachers to have greater skill in the evaluation of research that they read (Bain, Sager Brown, & Jordan, 2009). However, it is not the only determining factor as to which practices and/or resources teachers choose to adopt in their classrooms (Coldwell et al., 2017). Most teachers practice with a degree of adaptivity. That is, they must 'adjust their instruction in real-time to meet the specific needs of individual students or the demands of the situation in which they find themselves' (Parsons, Dodman, & Burrowbridge, 2013, p. 40). Evidence-informed teaching practice is, therefore, frequently recognised as complex and context-driven (Coldwell et al., 2017), comprising professional judgement in combination with robust evidence from research (Coldwell et al., 2017; Masters, 2018; Nelson & Campbell, 2017). Indeed, Sharples (2013) describes evidence-informed teaching practice in education as the integration of professional expertise with the best external research evidence. Nelson and Campbell (2017) expand on this and, echoing descriptions of teacher adaptivity above, acknowledge the pivotal role that professional judgement plays in the practice decisions made by teachers. Furthermore, Depp and Lebowitz (2007) emphasise that within clinical intervention trials, use of the intervention is not optional. It seems clear that educators operating in real-world contexts must decide on which practices they will choose over other available practices. It was, therefore, imperative that the Autism CRC School Years Program knowledge translation strategy was co-designed with educators and allied health professionals in order to capture teachers' insights into contextual challenges that influenced their decision-making when mobilising new knowledge into their practice. This strategy fits neatly with Marder and deBettencourt's (2015) acknowledgement of the importance of teacher judgement in the appropriate selection and implementation of teaching practices with their particular students.

All of the above highlights the complexity underpinning teachers' adoption of teaching practices and underscores the challenge for researchers working in the education field. It is important, therefore, for us to consider how we can help teachers to mobilise research knowledge into practice.

Mobilising research for use in the inclusive classroom context

It comes as little surprise that there is a great divide between discovering new or confirmatory evidence and the successful mobilisation of this evidence by classroom teachers into their practice, in their context, with their diverse group of students. Within this chapter, we have adopted the term 'knowledge mobilisation' in recognition that in and of itself, knowledge cannot inform or influence educational practices simply because it is 'available'. This is not to suggest that teachers are the only potential users of our research. As Read, Cooper, Edelstein, Sohn, and Levin (2013) identify:

> research knowledge is mobilised effectively when organizational leaders, practitioners, policy makers and researchers from different institutions and contexts learn together using research to inform thinking and professional practice.
>
> (p. 25)

Knowledge mobilisation cannot therefore occur within a bubble of academia. Modifying practice, which is informed by research evidence, is reliant on interpretation by those who will use it (Coburn, Toure, & Yamashita, 2009) and this interpretation is fashioned by 'pre-existing beliefs and practices and day-to-day limits on how they [teachers] direct their attention' (Coburn, Honig, & Stein, 2009, p. 86). The knowledge translation strategy implemented as part of the Autism CRC School Years Program was particularly focused on successful adoption of new knowledge by Australian teachers in inclusive school settings and what influenced both teacher professional judgement and decisions about their practice.

It is clear that mobilisation of evidence into teaching practice is not a straightforward, linear transfer of researched practices for standardised use in the classroom by teachers (Levin, 2013). A paucity of support for teacher translation of evidence is described by Markle and Lamont (2013, p. 1): 'alarmingly few resources exist to help schools adapt the [evidence-based] practice to their specific needs and resources, plan their efforts, ensure fidelity to their plan, and evaluate their outcomes'. There are very few resources that exist to help teachers translate and mobilise research evidence to practice in their context, with their particular group of students. However, this was exactly the intention behind the School Years Program of the Autism CRC.

The Cooperative Research Centre for Living with Autism: The School Years Program

The Commonwealth of Australia's Co-operative Research Centre (CRC) program supports the development of research into problems and issues prioritised by end-users through genuine collaboration with researchers, industry partners, and end-users. Impactful research should be characterised by mutual engagement and co-production (Levin, 2013; Read et al., 2013; Watt, 2015) and this was certainly the focus in the Autism CRC School Years Program of research. The mission of the Autism CRC has been to 'Motivate, facilitate and translate collaborative autism research across the life-span, underpinned by inclusive practices' (Autism CRC, 2020) with the first research projects commissioned in 2013–2014. The overarching themes of the original Autism CRC School Years projects were determined through extensive consultation with end-users during the development stages of the Autism CRC and subsequently confirmed by the Autism CRC *Australian Autism Educational Needs Analysis* research project (Saggers et al., 2018). All projects were conducted under one of three themes: i) Enhancing learning, teaching, and the learning experience; ii) Social emotional wellbeing and school connectedness/engagement; and iii) Linking student experiences and developmental and behavioural trajectories. Research in the Autism CRC School Years Program has strived not only to be responsive to the needs of families, educators, and students on the spectrum but to produce research knowledge that impacts teaching and teaching practices in inclusive classrooms.

> *The focus of the Autism CRC School Years Program was on conducting research within schools and in classrooms, usually in partnership with educators, parents, and students.*

The focus of the Autism CRC School Years Program was on conducting research within schools and in classrooms, usually in partnership with educators, parents, and students. This ensured that researchers and school community stakeholders worked together to develop evidence-informed strategies and resources for inclusive classrooms. To continue these partnerships, the Autism CRC School Years Program wanted to provide Australian school communities with the means to mobilise the vast array of findings from a wide range of individual research projects. The belief was that in order to directly impact what teachers *do*, educational researchers must rely upon teachers to act as agents of the knowledge generated by their research. In so doing, teachers become critical enactors and mobilisers as opposed to passive recipients of research findings. Enabling teachers to actively engage with research findings relied on developing a comprehensive understanding of the needs and challenges faced by school communities and organisations.

In the previous chapter of this volume, Whelan, Kerr, Harper-Hill, and Zelenko describe the co-design process undertaken during the development of the online educational resource platform *inclusionED*.[1] If the platform was to enable educators to use the findings of the Autism CRC research projects to inform their practice, it needed to meet the professional learning needs of educators in inclusive school settings, understand their decision-making process, while also supporting them to meet the challenges they face 'on the ground'.

> ...*to directly impact what teachers do, educational researchers must rely upon teachers to act as agents of the knowledge generated by their research.*

The following section of the chapter explores two insights into the needs of teachers which were revealed from the ongoing relationship between researchers and teachers during the co-design journey.

Knowledge mobilisation: Meeting the needs of teachers

To support the development of *inclusionED* as an online platform, co-design research sessions were conducted with teachers. The teacher perspectives drawn from the transcripts of these co-design sessions (described in the previous chapter) were used to inform the design and development of the platform. The co-design phase was followed by usability testing of the platform prototype (Kerr, Zelenko, Whelan, Harper-Hill, & Villalba, submitted). Transcripts from these co-design and testing sessions were analysed and a number of findings, which were important to the perceived utility of new knowledge by teachers, were identified. These findings are particularly relevant to teacher judgement and decision-making.

The first fundamental finding was teachers' need for their professional learning to be supported by a community of practice with like-minded colleagues. As such, *inclusionED* was designed to operate not simply as a repository of research findings and tools for research translation, but as a community of practice. Situated as a community of practice, *inclusionED* is well placed to influence teacher decision-making with regard to trialing evidence-informed practice. As discussed earlier, the opportunity to trial evidence-informed practice certainly requires that teachers read and access research. Further, progression to adopting evidence-informed practice occurs after the opportunity to test it out but is strongly influenced by teachers' own observations of successful implementation of the practice in action and through recommendations made by trusted colleagues (Coldwell et al., 2017).

The design of *inclusionED* provides mechanisms through which all of these can be achieved. However, it was not the most compelling theme to emerge. Teachers clearly reported that they would be best supported if the platform could enable them to meet the needs of a range of students in their classroom.

Teachers indicated that diagnosis was not necessarily the primary consideration when responding to student need. The specialist teacher below described how a diagnosis ('sticky label') in isolation was insufficient to determine how to best meet the support needs of a student:

> … it doesn't matter what the sticky label is, but while an accurate diagnosis is important, what I'm actually saying to you is the level of what you're acting on, which is the basic adjustments and supports that are needed to enable this student to participate in what you're offering.
>
> (Support teacher, Usability-testing)

Teachers very clearly indicated that the value of a practice was influenced by whether they perceived that it could meet the needs of a range of students. The first of the quotes below reiterates that these needs were not necessarily restricted to those students with a diagnosis of autism.

> if you get it right for the students with autism you'll be getting it right … in the room in general. It's not just about getting changes for two or three. It's actually getting down to brass tacks more than you're actually doing, which is going to catch all the people that you're not aware of who aren't understanding what you're on about either.
>
> (Support teacher, Usability-testing)

> So that worked well for him [child with autism]: I also had my eye on another little boy who's highly intelligent, but hates anything to do with pencil/paper. I didn't break – didn't go through the whole process with him, but I gave him the adjusted assessment piece, which was enlarged, and broken up to pieces with lots of breaks. And another two boys asked if they could have the same one, so that gave access to other children too.
>
> (Classroom teacher, Co-design session)

Further, and echoing Green and Cherrington (2010), some of the teachers recognised specific, alternative sources of diversity but, again, it was student need which determined their practice:

> So when the children come to school, obviously they come from various backgrounds, and looking at the curriculum, there was a need in the curriculum that I needed to fill. It might be writing activities that could suit everybody in the class, or just general teaching.
>
> (Support teacher, Co-design session)

Similarly, recognising that some needs such as emotional regulation are frequently seen as a specific need for students on the spectrum does not preclude them from being a need that is shared by other students. For example:

> That regulation is core business for kids on the spectrum, and it should be part of our teaching and learning environment and their curriculum, but more than that, it actually should be part of the curriculum for all students …
> (Support teacher, Co-design session)

By being responsive to need, rather than diagnosis, teachers described practices which naturally extended to meet the needs of many students. In the example below, the teacher refers to an adjusted 'task' which has incorporated a range of adjustments informed by research:

> … I feel that a task like this would be, not just help that one child, it actually helps multiple children in the classroom. And I could see that, through the repetition of doing this activity with the other children. So that's why it was successful with the whole class. And individual students, but also had wider parameters.
> (Classroom teacher, Co-design session)

inclusionED as an online resource platform was therefore designed to be responsive to teachers, and practices were framed according to the educational needs that they supported, not simply through a lens of autism. When teachers spoke about how a practice or approach could meet the needs of many students, this was not restricted to students in their classroom. Teachers reported favourably on practices that could be effectively implemented across school communities:

> And we went back and we talked to staff in staff meetings about how we might be able to implement it, we trialled it … and it worked really well, with both junior school and senior school … this was something that kind of involved everybody having a go, and it was worthwhile sharing with all of them because they – it was applicable to all of them, instead of isolating a particular grade.
> (Support Teacher, Co-design session)

There were teacher participants in the co-design and usability testing sessions who explicitly reported that the impact of the research communicated on *inclusionED* would be negated if it did not, where appropriate, support teaching to the diversity in classroom contexts. As such, *inclusionED* was positioned to support teachers to respond to student need rather than the child's diagnosis. However, this was not without tension.

Primarily, the student participants in the research informing *inclusionED* were on the autism spectrum. Any observed benefits to participating students in the

> A diagnosis of autism can certainly signpost potential student need but these needs cannot be assumed and must be established in response to the strengths and challenges experienced by the individual student and identified through rigorous data collection.

individual research projects could not be generalised to their peers who were not on the autism spectrum. Similarly, however, the heterogeneity inherent between autistic students is well documented and, paradoxically, generalisation to all students on the basis of diagnosis could also not be assumed. A diagnosis of autism can certainly signpost potential student need but these needs cannot be assumed and must be established in response to the strengths and challenges experienced by the individual student and identified through rigorous data collection. In order to stay true to our commitment to teachers as agents of our research findings, there was just cause to meet the needs of teachers by enabling them to meet the needs of many students, not only those on the autism spectrum.

Teacher feedback also clearly articulated the need to have confidence that the teaching practices they learned about were underpinned by sound evidence. Reflecting that teaching is a *practice* (e.g., Kemmis, 2014; Shulman, 2005), each research project team from the Autism CRC School Years Program generated at least one evidence-informed practice for teachers to adopt. Several of the projects generated many more, with one of these, the Transition Models of Practice, generating in excess of 50 evidence-informed practices for teachers to access and implement. The *inclusionED* research team sought additional, and independent, feedback to support the research evidence for the various teaching practices that were developed in the School Years Program and a collaboration with the Evidence for Learning website[2] was undertaken.

The aim was to provide independent evaluation of the objective evidence underpinning the practices presented on the *inclusionED* platform. These evidence summaries, referred to as 'toolkits', allocate each practice to a pre-existing category of practices and report on the available evidence underpinning each category of practice. This evidence is concerned with whether the evidence supports claims that a practice belonging to the category will *directly improve learning outcomes for students*.

Evidence for Learning summaries are determined by the quantity of evidence available and the quality of the methods used (including the outcomes measured) in the various research projects which generated the evidence. Where possible, the consistency with which various reviews and meta-analyses estimated the impact of practices is included in the ratings of evidence. Inevitably, the total available evidence on the efficacy and effectiveness of a practice to directly improve student learning outcomes and the quality of this underpinning research means that not all practices receive a high rating. We carefully considered the justification for including those practices with a lower rating of evidence for direct impact on student learning, as evaluated through the Evidence for Learning site. To do this, we returned to the key aims of the Autism CRC School Years Program.

Consistent with the commission by the Commonwealth Government of Australia, one aim of the Autism CRC School Years Program was to improve academic outcomes; however, the three themes of the School Years Program clearly demonstrate a broader remit. Classroom practices, environments, cultures, and approaches which would improve not only academic achievement but also the learning *experience* of students on the spectrum and ultimately their social emotional wellbeing were paramount. Including only those practices which met the most stringent of evidence ratings for improving learning attainment would restrict teachers from learning about practices which were informed or supported by the research more broadly. In light of this, practices put forward by researchers on the basis of the extended literature and their own expertise were included and the evidence described in a transparent way. Meeting the needs of teachers and researchers was a thorny affair which required us to revisit the aims and the ethos of the Autism CRC School Years Program which was to significantly and positively impact the lives of students on the spectrum, their families, and Australian teachers and schools. It is important to consider how we support researchers in mobilising the knowledge that is developed from their research.

Knowledge mobilisation: Meeting the needs of researchers

The second and equally critical component to optimal knowledge mobilisation through *inclusionED* was the way in which the *inclusionED* platform supports researchers to efficiently translate their findings for teachers. Identifying those design factors which led researchers to successfully create and upload content onto *inclusionED* can inform collaborative research efforts in the future.

From the outset, the commitment of the Autism CRC to knowledge mobilisation was explicit:

> We can only transform lives if there is effective translation and utilisation of research outcomes. Translation is a core consideration in the definition, development and validation of our research outputs.
>
> (Autism CRC, n.d., p. 4)

It is our belief that, while individual researcher teams in co-operative research centres are supported with funding, they are fiscal *custodians* with ongoing responsibility to keep knowledge mobilisation front and centre. As such, researchers must maintain productive partnerships with likely users and beneficiaries of their research in order that it will address the users' needs. Rather than viewing knowledge mobilisation as an obligatory 'add on' at the conclusion of a project, our approach requires researchers to anticipate and plan for knowledge mobilisation at project conceptualisation. Researchers must anticipate how their research will contribute to such evidence-informed

> ...while individual researcher teams in co-operative research centres are supported with funding, they are fiscal custodians with ongoing responsibility to keep knowledge mobilisation front and centre.

developments and be prepared to communicate these in a way which will support educators who are striving to implement evidence-informed practice.

It has been mooted that one of the barriers to knowledge mobilisation is the lack of institutional support and funding (Read et al., 2013). The Autism CRC demonstrated their strong commitment to knowledge mobilisation by establishing a specific project funding category called 'utilisation' projects. While the initial, individual utilisation projects produced high-quality teacher resources, research teams still required an efficient mechanism to upload both project content and practice resources that would result in extensive reach and maximum traction. To achieve this, the need for a whole-of-program knowledge translation strategy was recognised and this was ultimately realised through *inclusionED*.

The research which informed the design of the *inclusionED* platform began after the initial projects had begun and, in some cases, these projects were in the final stages of completion. Completed projects had developed resources informed by their findings and these were transferred to *inclusionED* although retrofitting resources to *inclusionED* was time-intensive and challenging. An iterative series of trials was undertaken to develop a research translation toolkit to support researchers in the quest to efficiently and effectively translate the findings from their research projects to classroom teachers in inclusive schools. The primary focus of each trial has been to scaffold researchers' efforts to mobilise findings according to the design and communication principles identified during the series of co-design activities and teacher consultations described in Chapter 5. A range of support tools have been developed to support researchers to conceptualise their research from a classroom delivery perspective.

RESEARCHER PERSPECTIVE

inclusionED has significantly increased the impact and reach of my research. It has done this by giving me a truly interactive, online platform where I can easily break down my research into smaller chunks for presentation in a format used by teachers in their everyday teaching. This includes a Core Research Platform for presenting my research summaries and Practice Modules for translating my research into the plans, goals, and resource requirements needed for teachers to apply my research in their classrooms. For me as a researcher, inclusionED is not just another repository for my research; it is a platform that directly translates my research into something that really does help real teachers in real classrooms.

Chief investigator of a research project which generated two *inclusionED* practices. In the three months following the *inclusionED* launch, one of these practices had been viewed 3,135 times.

Lessons from *inclusionED*: Implications for future research organisations

Dissemination of findings does not equate to research impact and, in Australia, there is increased pressure for researchers to demonstrate environmental, economic, and/or social impact of, and benefit from, their research to justify the investment (Australian Research Council, 2019). Despite the important contribution of research to improved student outcomes, the means by which knowledge is mobilised remains a point of debate for researchers (Read et al., 2013).

RESEARCHER PERSPECTIVE

Research in the field of autism practice (i.e., programs, supports, and services) is directed towards improving outcomes for people on the autism spectrum. Should a study demonstrate positive outcomes for its participants, the challenge for researchers is how to translate and embed the outcomes into everyday practice.

For researchers involved in the ACRC [Autism CRC] Models of Practice (MoP) educational research project, this challenge has been resolved with the establishment of inclusionED. inclusionED, an online professional learning community, will share the co-produced evidence-based teaching resources and strategies arising from the MoP with educators and parents from across Australia and result in better educational support for school-age students on the autism spectrum.

Chief investigator of a research project which generated in excess of 50 practices. In the three months following the *inclusionED* launch, one of these practices had been viewed 2,996 times.

The design and development of *inclusionED* was a program-wide response to the challenge of mobilising the knowledge generated from multiple research projects. It is not feasible, nor prudent, for every research project to attempt to generate the equivalent of the *inclusionED* platform. However, research which is motivated to support teacher practice must plan for, and attend to, the process of knowledge mobilisation. Successful mobilisation of knowledge in the classroom requires a genuine and shared partnership between researchers and teachers. It is therefore important to consider strategies for knowledge mobilisation in planning phases in research design and budget.

The *inclusionED* experience of supporting researchers to upload new research findings into a format that meets the needs of teachers delivers two key messages for maximising research impact. The first of these is that researchers are not equally equipped to design, develop, and produce digital resources and communications which engage those who will use their findings. Nor should they be. Production of such communications requires dedicated and experienced support, capacity building, and resourcing in a team-based environment including researchers, educators, and learning designers.

The second of these is the consideration of knowledge mobilisation strategies at a project design and submission stage. Research project design requires conceptualisation of possible knowledge mobilisation outputs in addition to those traditional academic outputs such as journal articles. Collaborative research partnerships between researchers and end-users such as teachers will ensure research can have a greater impact and support a more inclusive approach to education.

Notes

1 www.inclusioned.edu.au
2 https://evidenceforlearning.org.au

References

Australian Research Council. (2019). *Research impact principles and framework*. Retrieved from https://www.arc.gov.au/policies-strategies/strategy/research-impact-principles-framework.

Autism CRC. (n.d.). *Cooperative Research Centre for Living with Autism (Autism CRC)*. Brisbane: Cooperative Research Centre for Living with Autism (Autism CRC).

Autism CRC. (2020). *Cooperative Research Centre for Living with Autism (Autism CRC)* [website]. Retrieved from https://www.autismcrc.com.au/.

Bain, S. K., Sager Brown, K., & Jordan, K. R. (2009). Teacher candidates' accuracy of beliefs regarding childhood interventions. *The Teacher Educator*, 44(2), 71–89. doi:10.1080/08878730902755523.

Callahan, K., Hughes, H., Mehta, S., Toussaint, K., Nichols, S., Ma, P., … Wang, H. (2017). Social validity of evidence-based practices and emerging interventions in autism. *Focus on Autism and Other Developmental Disabilities*, 32(3), 188–197. doi:10.1177/1088357616632446.

Coburn, C., Honig, M., & Stein, M. (2009). What's the evidence on districts' use of evidence? In J. Bransford, D. Stipek, N. Vye, L. Gomez, & D. Lam (Eds.), *The role of research in educational improvement* (pp. 67–87). Cambridge, MA: Harvard Education Press.

Coburn, C., Toure, J., & Yamashita, M. (2009). Evidence, interpretation, and persuasion: Instructional decision making at the district central office. *Teachers College Record*, 111(4), 1115–1161.

Coldwell, M., Greany, T., Higgins, S., Brown, C., Maxwell, B., Stiell, B., … Burns, H. (2017). *Evidence-informed teaching: An evaluation of progress in England*. London: Department for Education. Retrieved from https://assets.publishing.service.gov.uk/government/uploads/system/uploads/attachment_data/file/625007/Evidence-informed_teaching_-_an_evaluation_of_progress_in_England.pdf.

Depp, C., & Lebowitz, B. D. (2007). Clinical trials: Bridging the gap between efficacy and effectiveness. *International Review of Psychiatry*, 19(5), 531–539. doi:10.1080/09540260701563320.

Good, T. (2008). *21st century education: A reference handbook*. Thousand Oaks, CA: SAGE.

Green, A., & Stormont, M. (2018). Creating culturally responsive and evidence-based lessons for diverse learners with disabilities. *Intervention in School and Clinic*, 53(3), 138–145. doi:10.1177/1053451217702114.

Green, V., & Cherrington, S. (2010). *Delving into diversity: An international exploration of issues of diversity in education*. New York, NY: Nova Science Publishers.

Kemmis, S. (2014). Praxis, practice and practice architectures. In S. Kemmis, J. Wilkinson, C. Edwards-Groves, I. Hardy, P. Grootenboer, & Bristol, L (Eds.), *Changing practices, changing education* (pp. 25–41). Singapore: Springer Singapore. doi:10.1007/978-981-4560-47-4.

Kerr, J., Zelenko, O., Whelan, M., Harper-Hill, K., & Villalba, C. (submitted). *A model for co-designing with multiple stakeholder groups from the 'fuzzy' front-end to beyond project delivery: Designing inclusionED* [Manuscript submitted for publication]. Brisbane: Creative Industries Faculty, Queensland University of Technology.

Levin, B. (2013). To know is not enough: Research knowledge and its use. *Review of Education*, 1(1), 2–31. doi:10.1002/rev3.3001.

Luiselli, J. K., & Reed, D. D. (2011). Social validity. In S. Goldstein & J. A. Naglieri (Eds.), *Encyclopedia of child behavior and development* (p. 1406). Boston, MA: Springer. doi:10.1007/978-0-387-79061-9_3168.

Marder, T., & deBettencourt, L. U. (2015). Teaching students with ASD using evidence-based practices: Why is training critical now? *Teacher Education and Special Education*, 38(1), 5–12. doi:10.1177/0888406414565838.

Markle, R. S., & Lamont, A. E. (2013). A guide for ensuring quality implementation of evidence-based practices in schools. *Communiqué*, 41(7), 1, 25–28.

Masters, G. (2018). The role of evidence in teaching and learning. *Teacher*. Retrieved from: https://www.teachermagazine.com.au/columnists/geoff-masters/the-role-of-evidence-in-teaching-and-learning.

Nelson, J., & Campbell, C. (2017). Evidence-informed practice in education: Meanings and applications. *Educational Research*, 59(2), 127–135. doi:10.1080/00131881.2017.1314115.

Parsons, S. A., Dodman, S. L., & Burrowbridge, S. C. (2013). Broadening the view of differentiated instruction. *Phi Delta Kappan*, 95(1), 38–42. doi:10.1177/003172171309500107.

Read, R., Cooper, A., Edelstein, H., Sohn, J., & Levin, B. (2013). Knowledge mobilisation and utilisation. In B. Levin, J. Qi, H. Edelstein, & J. Sohn (Eds.), *The impact of research in education: An international perspective* (pp. 23–39). Bristol: The Policy Press.

Saggers, B., Klug, D., Harper-Hill, K., Ashburner, J., Costley, D., Clark, T., … Carrington, S. (2018). *Australian autism educational needs analysis: What are the needs of schools, parents and students on the autism spectrum?* Brisbane: Cooperative Research Centre for Living with Autism (Autism CRC).

Saggers, B., Tones, M., Dunne, J., & Aberdein, R. (2019). Tele-classroom consultation: Promoting an inclusive approach to supporting the needs of educators, families and early years learners on the autism spectrum in rural and remote areas in contextually responsive ways. *International Journal of Inclusive Education*. doi:10.1080/13603116.2019.1609103.

Sharples, J. (2013). *Evidence for the frontline. A report for the Alliance for Useful Evidence*. Retrieved from http://www.alliance4usefulevidence.org/assets/EVIDENCE-FOR-THE-FRONTLINE-FINAL-5-June-2013.pdf.

Shulman, L. S. (2005). Signature pedagogies in the professions. *Daedalus*, 134(3), 52–59.

Watt, I. J. (2015). *Review of research policy and funding arrangements*. Retrieved from https://docs.education.gov.au/system/files/doc/other/main_report_final_20160112.pdf.

7
DEVELOPING COMMUNITIES OF PRACTICE FOR EDUCATOR PROFESSIONAL LEARNING

Developing connections in rural and remote regions

Chris Edwards and Beth Saggers

> This chapter continues the focus on knowledge mobilisation by reporting on research that explored the role played by communities of practice (CoP) in supporting school communities to translate research knowledge into practice in contextually responsive ways. The focus of this research was on supporting school communities in rural and remote regions of Australia using a novel tele-classroom consultation approach to support a CoP within the school community. School-based CoPs provide an opportunity for ongoing collaborative approaches to be sustained that support the adoption of inclusive practices by all members of a school community. Successful CoPs can give educators, families, and students a sense of belonging and build positive relationships. The novel approach of using a tele-classroom consultation to facilitate a CoP in rural and remote regions can overcome many difficulties experienced by educators in these regions in receiving ongoing and contextually relevant professional learning that is responsive to their needs.

Educators can experience challenges meeting the needs of learners on the spectrum in inclusive settings (Brunsting, Sreckovic, & Lane, 2014). A recent Australian study exploring the educational needs of learners on the autism spectrum found that educators, specialists, and parents ($N = 1,468$) highlighted the importance of additional education and training to help support educators with these challenges (Saggers et al., 2018). Educators in rural and remote settings often experience additional challenges and complexities compared to their urban counterparts (Glover et al., 2016; Halsey, 2018), one of the most prevalent issues being the personal and professional isolation they experience through geographic location. In addition, many educators in rural and remote regions are newly qualified professionals completing their first years as qualified teachers, often increasing their feelings of personal and professional isolation (Kline & Walker-Gibbs, 2015). Limited professional learning opportunities, minimal/outdated educational resources, and restricted networking opportunities can often further disadvantage rural and remote educators (Glover et al., 2016).

Communities of practice (CoPs) have been widely used in the field of education and are one approach that has been used to support the knowledge and skill set of educators in rural and remote regions, strengthening their ability to overcome these challenges (Vescio, Ross, & Adams, 2008; Walton, Carrington, Saggers, Edwards, & Kimani, 2019; Wenger, McDermott, & Snyder, 2002). A brief discussion of CoPs will now be provided, before introducing a model of service delivery that can support CoPs in rural and remote regions. This model of service delivery was termed the tele-classroom consultation approach and was developed as part of the Autism CRC Early Years Behaviour Support Project (EYBSP).

What are communities of practice?

As part of their exploration of situated learning, anthropologists Lave and Wenger (1991) were the first to coin the concept 'communities of practice'. More recently CoPs have been described as 'groups of people who share a concern, a set of problems, or a passion about a topic, and who deepen their knowledge and expertise in this area by interacting on an ongoing basis' (Wenger et al., 2002, p. 4). A CoP can be conceptualised as a balance between three interrelated elements: i) Domain; ii) Community; and iii) Practice (Wenger et al., 2002) as shown in Figure 7.1. These are described as follows:

- The **Domain** is the shared interest that unites community members around a common interest or goal.

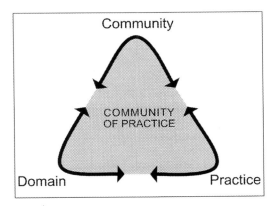

FIGURE 7.1 Communities of practice: Conceptual diagram.
Source: Edwards, 2019; adapted from Wenger et al., 2002.

- The **Community** refers to the members that actively collaborate in joint activities.
- The **Practices** can be described as a shared set of resources, skills, and actions that the Community utilises to support their Domain.

> As a result of active participation within a CoP, members are likely to develop various short-term values (Wenger et al., 2002). Short-term values identified by Wenger et al. (2002) include:
>
> - Overcoming challenges.
> - Accessing expertise.
> - Developing better teamwork.
> - Increasing confidence.
> - Increasing enjoyment.
> - Meaningful participation.

One approach that can be used to support a CoP is teleconsultation. This is a novel approach that is increasingly being used to overcome geographical limitations in rural and remote regions and to deliver professional development (Bice-Urbach & Kratochwill, 2016).

Teleconsultation as an alternate service delivery option

Teleconsultation is a flexible mode of service delivery that utilises information and communication technology to connect consultant(s) with consultee(s) through an interactive video and/or audio medium (Hepburn, Blakeley-Smith, Wolff, & Reaven, 2016). It is the flexibility that teleconsultation can provide that can be used to overcome many of the professional learning challenges experienced in rural and remote communities. Teleconsultation is a model of service delivery that can provide professional development that is cost-effective while also delivering real-time support and feedback to staff in geographically remote areas (Frieder, Peterson, Woodward, Crane, & Garner, 2009). To date, teleconsultation has been widely applied within the health sector with successful outcomes in delivering a range of cost-effective health and allied health services (American Psychiatric Association [APA], 2013; Brownlee, Graham, Doucette, Hotson, & Halverson, 2010; Frieder et al., 2009; Hepburn et al., 2016) but with limited applications in education. Some initial key studies, however, have presented promising results in the education sector for the use of teleconsultation to connect knowledgeable consultants with parents, therapists, and educators of learners on the spectrum in rural and remote regions (Bice-Urbach & Kratochwill, 2016; Lindgren et al., 2016; Saggers, Tones, Dunne, & Aberdein, 2019).

The Autism CRC *Australian Autism Educational Needs Analysis* (ASD–ENA; Saggers et al., 2018) provided valuable insight into the perceptions of educators and specialists regarding the use of teleconsultation to support the needs of learners on the spectrum.

> In the nationwide survey, educators and specialists agreed on the following four key benefits to using teleconsultation:
>
> - Reduction of travel time and costs for additional support.
> - Increased access and support to services.
> - Improved school-based access to specialist support and services.
> - Increased liaison and collaboration between specialist support and school-based staff.

Teleconsultation to support communities of practice

While teleconsultation has been justified as a cost-effective service delivery model in education, there is minimal research to support its use to develop and sustain CoPs within education communities (e.g., Barker, Mallow, Theeke, & Schwertfeger, 2016; Maher & Prescott, 2017; Trust & Horrocks, 2017; Zournazis & Marlow, 2015). With research suggesting CoPs can overcome many challenges educators in rural and remote regions experience supporting learners on the spectrum, teleconsultation can provide access to a novel service delivery option to support these CoPs (Laluvein, 2010). This chapter focuses on research investigating the use of a teleconsultation approach to support CoPs to meet the professional learning needs of educators working with learners on the autism spectrum in rural and remote regions of Australia.

Introduction to the larger Autism CRC EYBSP research project

This chapter reports on a Doctor of Philosophy (PhD) research project that was conducted as part of a larger national research study, the Autism CRC Early Years Behaviour Support Project (EYBSP). The larger research project recruited five rural and remote mainstream Australian schools who wanted additional support to better meet the needs of young learners on the autism spectrum in their care. All five schools trialled teleconsultation as a novel research approach to support their professional development and, in turn, meet the needs of learners on the spectrum in their school contexts.

Tele-classroom consultation approach developed as part of the EYBSP research project

The larger EYBSP research project developed a teleconsultation-based support model described as a tele-classroom consultation (TCC) approach (Saggers et al., 2019). This approach utilised a combination of face-to-face and teleconsultation-based

> *The purpose of the TCC approach was to provide ongoing assistance and support that was tailored to the contextual and individual needs of the learners, families, educators, and schools.*

support to connect a multidisciplinary team of therapists, teachers, and specialist support staff (from an autism-specific service provider) to a range of school staff (Saggers et al., 2019). The purpose of the TCC approach was to provide ongoing assistance and support that was tailored to the contextual and individual needs of the learners, families, educators, and schools. The ongoing support and feedback focused on better equipping school staff with the skills and knowledge to implement contextually relevant and sustainable school-wide adjustments. Given the flexibility within the approach, support was provided through various teleconsultation-based delivery modes tailored to the preferences of the participants, such as Zoom video software, emails, and phone calls. A brief summary of the approach has been presented in Table 7.1.

The PhD project: Part of the larger study

As part of the larger EYBSP research project, a PhD research project explored how this innovative model of support could promote CoPs for school staff in two of the five schools, and assist them to overcome contextually relevant challenges. It is the results from this PhD research that is the focus of this chapter. This chapter is co-authored by the EYBSP project leader and the PhD researcher.

Within the two nominated schools, a multidisciplinary team from a metropolitan autism-specific service provider employed a TCC approach across a school year to help educators in these schools to support the needs of learners on the autism spectrum. The team consisted of a professional learning facilitator, an occupational therapist, and speech–language pathologist. The team visited the schools at the beginning of the project to assess the needs of the learners and the school communities and to gain a better understanding of the contexts. They worked with the school communities to identify what support was needed, then developed a plan for implementing and delivering this support through the TCC approach. The findings provide insight into how the CoPs were supported as a result of the TCC approach.

Methodology

As CoPs explore a complex social phenomenon, educational research on CoPs as a concept supports the use of qualitative methods of research (Cuddapah & Clayton, 2011; Wilson, Delbridge, & Palermo, 2017). In the current research, a qualitative approach provided the researchers with the ability and flexibility to explore the phenomenon in depth, drawing on rich detail from multiple sources in order to strengthen the contextual understanding (Creswell, 2003). There are varying approaches to educational case studies and for the purpose of the PhD research, an exploratory multiple case study was adopted (Yin, 2003). This exploration allowed both cases to be individually analysed in detail, while also conducting

TABLE 7.1 Summary of the Tele-Classroom Consultation Approach

TCC component	Summary
Understanding context	Initial contact made with families and schools. Initial face-to-face consultation with support team to identify contextual and individual needs of learners, families, educators, and schools.
Autism-specific multidisciplinary support team	Speech–language pathologist. Occupational therapist. Professional learning facilitator. Indigenous liaison officer (to promote cultural safety of support provided to one school that included a learner from an Indigenous background).
Stages of the TCC approach	**Assessment**: The contextual needs of the learners, families, educators, and school were assessed. **Preparation**: The TCC approach and support plan were co-created with the school staff. **Implementation of support**: Support model implemented across a school year, with periodic evaluations and revisions made as part of the process. **Post-implementation**: To promote sustainability, a follow-up and exit plan were co-developed with school staff.
Face-to-face visits	**Frequency**: Initial visit, with four follow-up face-to-face visits (one per school term). **Purpose**: • To unite key stakeholders and understand their contextual and individual needs. • To build rapport and trust, while strengthening communication networks.
Teleconsultation sessions	**Frequency**: Frequency and delivery of teleconsultation sessions guided by preferences of school staff, ensuring sessions were responsive and flexible to their needs. **Purpose**: • To provide real-time contextually relevant feedback and support convenient to school staff. • To strengthen relationships established through face-to-face visits.

Source: Adapted from Saggers et al. (2019).

a cross-case analysis. The overarching question that guided the PhD research was: To what extent can a TCC approach support a CoP for educators in rural and remote regions supporting the complex needs of children on the spectrum in the early years?

Both schools (Charlie School and Echo School[1]) involved in the project were government schools in rural and remote regions of Queensland, Australia. The staff at the schools nominated to be involved in the research due to challenges they were experiencing meeting the individual needs of a specific learner on the spectrum at their school. While both schools were in outer regional areas of Queensland, there were notable differences between the two school contexts including the size of the schools, and the large Indigenous population within Echo School (with the learner in Echo School coming from an Indigenous background). Charlie School was a very small school with a teaching principal and 11 students enrolled from Prep to Year 6, while Echo School had 11 staff and 92 students from Prep to Year 12.

The research participants included the multidisciplinary support team as well as the educators that were involved in supporting their respective learner on the spectrum within each school. The TCC approach was supported across one school year and data were collected and analysed at both pre-implementation and post-implementation stages (approximately 12 months apart). While it was not possible in the research time frame to explore the long-term values and sustainability of the CoPs, the post-implementation findings provided insight into the short-term values of the research. Data collection included observations of key face-to-face discussions between the support team and relevant educators in order to identify through a detailed observation protocol, relevant CoP elements. In addition, one-on-one semi-structured phone interviews were conducted with participants, guided by an interview protocol that was structured around the CoP elements. Data were triangulated from interviews and observations to strengthen the trustworthiness of the information (Gibson & Brown, 2009). The triangulated data provided insight into how a CoP evolved within each school.

What were the key findings?

A cross-case comparison of individual school findings provides valuable insight into how the TCC approach supported CoPs in these two different school contexts. The key findings will be structured around the CoP elements of Domain, Community, and Practice, and short-term values that evolved.

Domain

The Domain refers to the shared goal that members within a CoP strive to achieve (Wenger et al., 2002). Initially, stakeholders were united to reduce restrictive practices and promote inclusive practices to provide a better learning environment for all of their learners. Throughout the TCC approach, this shared vision was progressively strengthened by the support team and school staff. As a result, the shared goal of promoting inclusion evolved as their CoPs developed to become more specific, contextual, and achievable.

> ...the shared goal of promoting inclusion evolved as their CoPs developed to become more specific, contextual, and achievable.

The TCC approach promoted this collective vision through the combination of face-to-face visits and the delivery of teleconsultation support on a regular basis. The face-to-face meetings that took place once a term throughout the school year were reinforced by the support team and school staff. They shared the same overarching vision for inclusion, while the flexibility of the teleconsultation support ensured that specific and measurable goals were progressively achieved throughout the year.

As a consequence of this flexibility, school staff became more engaged and proactive in how they supported their inclusive environments. In fact, many school staff went above and beyond their position description to proactively seek additional support and educational resources to achieve their goals. Similarly, the support team felt that the TCC approach greatly increased the awareness and ability of school staff to proactively promote inclusive education. More importantly, it promoted inclusion relative to their contextual requirements. As a result, the TCC approach supported school staff in promoting and achieving a clear vision for inclusive education within their schools.

Community

The Community element within a CoP includes the members that actively collaborate and communicate to support and achieve their Domain (Wenger et al., 2002). Parallel to the development of the Domain, the TCC approach strengthened the Community element of the CoP in these regional Australian schools. Guided by a shared vision moving forward, the combination of face-to-face visits and flexible teleconsultation delivery options fostered growth within the Community. This was evident through the quality of the relationships that developed between the support team and school staff throughout the TCC approach. Similarly, this was also evident within the internal relationships that developed within the schools.

The TCC approach supported the Community element through these flexible and adaptive communication modes. This flexibility promoted ongoing two-way communication between the support team and school staff. Furthermore, it connected the school staff with a knowledgeable, multidisciplinary support team that they could reach out to at their convenience. However, it was more than just convenience, as school staff were supported with contextually relevant feedback that empowered them to adopt more inclusive practices within their school. As a result, the TCC approach promoted channels for communication, strengthened relationships, and provided contextually relevant support, supporting knowledge mobilisation for the CoP and developing the Community element.

Practices

According to Wenger et al. (2002), the Practices within a CoP refer to a shared set of tools such as resources, activities, practices, strategies, and techniques that the Community can utilise to achieve their shared goal. As the TCC approach strengthened the Domain and Community elements, a shared set of evidence-based and contextually relevant inclusive practices became more evident within these schools. How were these Practices developed throughout the TCC approach?

Many educators in rural and remote regions often need access to more knowledge and skills in order to effectively support learners on the autism spectrum (Glover et al., 2016; Halsey, 2018; Saggers et al., 2018). The multidisciplinary support team were able to provide education and training to school staff, to better equip them with this content knowledge. More importantly, they supported the school staff with knowledge and expertise relevant to their context and the specific learning needs of their learners on the spectrum that increased knowledge mobilisation and knowledge translation.

The CoP provided the opportunity for school staff to further develop their professional skills so that they were better able to meet the needs of learners on the autism spectrum in their care, within an inclusive learning environment. Through this deeper level of understanding, developed as part of the CoP, school staff became more proactive in sharing evidence-based knowledge and teaching practices. Similarly, school staff became more flexible and responsive to the contextual needs within their environment.

Short-term values

The flexible communication options supported school staff with contextually relevant support and feedback as they were encouraged to take advantage of the opportunity to reach out to a multidisciplinary support team. One short-term value that was evident as a result of the research was that the professional knowledge of school staff was nurtured over a 12-month period as they were supported to overcome a diverse range of contextually relevant challenges and this helped them translate the knowledge into practice.

Another key professional learning outcome that school staff experienced was their comprehensive growth in confidence. An increase in confidence both inside and outside the classroom was consistently reported by the support team and school staff. School staff were more confident in their own knowledge, ability, judgement, and teaching practices to support their learners on the spectrum. More importantly, they became more confident in their ability to create inclusive learning environments and to overcome contextually relevant challenges that they may face in the future.

> School staff were more confident in their own knowledge, ability, judgement, and teaching practices to support their learners on the spectrum.

Implications for inclusive education practice

In educational research, it is important to consider how the learnings can be used to mobilise educator knowledge of inclusion and support school staff and researchers in promoting and implementing inclusive education. Some key implications from this research are now described.

Balance of face-to-face and teleconsultation

Despite the wealth of evidence supporting teleconsultation as an effective delivery option for health-related services, the current research promotes its application in education settings. Results of this research suggest that when employing a TCC approach in schools, a combination of both face-to-face and more remote consultations is key. This aligns with emerging educational literature that face-to-face time is an essential component of an educational teleconsultation-based approach (Saggers et al., 2019). Rural and remote schools often operate in a complex environment, with further challenges arising through supporting learners on the spectrum (Saggers et al., 2018). Given the complexities that can exist in these regions, face-to-face time is critical to establishing rapport and establishing working collaborative relationships between any support team and school staff. As discussed earlier, relationships as part of the Community element of a CoP are a foundational component. Furthermore, face-to-face time also contributes to the rich understanding of the context-specific needs of the environment for each learner including the needs of the staff, parents, and the environment involved. It is through this contextualised understanding that the support team in collaboration with school staff is able to individualise the approach to the specific learning needs of each learner and help staff mobilise and translate the professional learning in context-specific ways. Therefore, this research strongly aligned with emerging educational literature that emphasises the significant role of face-to-face time being embedded in a teleconsultation approach, in particular to support CoPs.

Communication is key

As discussed throughout this chapter, communication is essential to promoting the Community element, and ultimately the CoP (Wenger et al., 2002). The TCC approach promoted communication by supporting relationships over the school year and by providing school staff with various opportunities to communicate internally and externally. Importantly, the approach was tailored to the preferences of school staff. For example, in many instances, school staff were interested in email communication as it meant that they could read and respond at their convenience. In other cases, phone calls or online meetings were suitable where an educator was eager to collaborate around a real-time challenge or issue. The key implication here is that the TCC approach was responsive and flexible, adapting to the varying communication preferences expressed by school staff, thereby strengthening the Community and overall CoP.

> *The TCC approach promoted communication by supporting relationships over the school year and by providing school staff with various opportunities to communicate internally and externally.*

Relationship of communities of practice elements

Many professional learning programs have focused on shaping and adapting the teaching practices of school staff (e.g., Christ & Wang, 2013). Nearly 20 years ago, Guskey (2002) argued that educators are more likely to adapt and change their teaching practices when they can see and measure the outcomes of their changes within their students and see a positive influence on their students. Over the years, this model for professional learning has been supported by rigorous educational research (e.g., Desimone, 2009; Opfer & Pedder, 2010).

The present research aligned with Guskey's (2002) model for professional learning and extended it further in relation to supporting CoPs. While the end goal was to support a shared set of evidence-based inclusive practices (Practices), the Domain and Community elements played a significant role in shaping these Practices. For instance, the face-to-face time, embedded with frequent communication through teleconsultation delivery options, strengthened and clarified the overarching goal, the Domain. Furthermore, the constant communication embedded throughout this flexible delivery promoted the internal and external relationships, the Community element. As a result, the Domain and Community elements were foundational to supporting educators as they adapted their Practices and developed professionally within the CoP.

Community of practice development is gradual

While previous practical implications presented how this research can support school staff and researchers in developing similar CoPs, arguably the most significant factor to consider here is that CoPs are not a 'quick fix'. Traditionally, the professional learning of educators has been conducted through face-to-face workshops and/or short courses, options that are both challenging and expensive for educators based in rural and remote locations (ElShaer, Calabrese, Casanova, & Huet, 2016; Wilson et al., 2017). Given the focus of a CoP is to promote long-term sustainability within a community, it needs to be recognised that they require considerable time and effort to not only establish, but to maintain. This was evident within the present research. These two schools were supported over a 12-month period, with their short-term values being explored at the end of the project. Due to the project timeframe, there was no opportunity to explore the long-term values as a follow-up phase. While 12 months may sound like a lengthy professional learning program for educators, it further highlights how gradually CoPs develop.

> Given the focus of a CoP is to promote long-term sustainability within a community, it needs to be recognised that they require considerable time and effort to not only establish, but to maintain.

More importantly, it emphasises how an investment into this level of time and effort can build sustainability in a community of educators.

Implications for inclusive education policy

The findings from this research have clear implications for inclusive education policy. Important considerations for future policy development including context, whole-school professional learning, supporting a national focus on rural and remote educators, and ensuring sustainable outcomes need to be considered.

The role of context in supporting communities of practice through teleconsultation

The golden thread interweaved throughout this chapter is the role of contextual understanding. Context is an essential factor that should be considered in promoting inclusive education, particularly for learners on the autism spectrum, as they can experience a diverse range of learning needs (Saggers et al., 2018; Walton et al., 2019). This innovative TCC approach differed from traditional professional learning programs, combining evidence-based concepts from telehealth and educational research (Hepburn et al., 2016; Saggers et al., 2019; Trust & Horrocks, 2017). However, the key factor that supported the effectiveness of this approach is how the multidisciplinary support team was supported with contextually relevant information within the approach.

Professional learning for educators is a school-wide topic

The TCC approach utilised within this research supported school staff who played a direct role in supporting their learners on the spectrum (e.g., classroom teacher, principal, teacher aides). While this was beneficial, it needs to be recognised that professional learning to promote inclusive learning environments is significant for the whole school, not just specific school staff. This is particularly relevant for rural and remote regions where educators experience various challenges that can increase their risk of turnover (Glover et al., 2016). Furthermore, as students progress through their school years, it is essential that all potential school staff that may play a role in supporting them are equipped with consistent, evidence-based, and inclusive practices. While professional learning should be individualised for specific school staff, there are key factors that must be considered and embedded across the whole school. These considerations can mitigate the risk of turnovers, while promoting a more inclusive school environment.

Teleconsultation: Strengthening the national focus on rural and remote educators

Educational research has consistently identified that educators and students in rural and remote regions are disadvantaged across multiple domains compared to their metropolitan counterparts (Glover et al., 2016; Kline & Walker-Gibbs, 2015). This has been supported in the recent *Independent Review into Regional, Rural and Remote Education*, led by Emeritus Professor John Halsey (2018). Of all the research, information, considerations, and recommendations presented within this report, Halsey (2018) identified the most significant as the need for a shared national focus to promote better access, outcomes, and opportunities for educators and students in rural and remote regions.

The research within this chapter presents compelling evidence that teleconsultation is the service delivery option to strengthen this national focus. Teleconsultation has been supported as effective and cost efficient by a wealth of health-related literature in addition to emerging educational research (APA, 2013; Brownlee et al.,

2010; Frieder et al., 2009; Hepburn et al., 2016; Saggers et al., 2019). More importantly, it can provide a much-needed voice for educators and schools in rural and remote regions by connecting them to a range of knowledgeable support providers.

Communities of practice and sustainable outcomes

This chapter has emphasised that professional learning through a teleconsultation approach to support CoPs is more complex than simply targeting teaching practices (Practices). Considerations must be taken to strengthen the shared goal (Domain) between community members (Community). This is the aspect that requires a considerable investment of time and effort from both the support team and school staff. Through this investment, the CoP can be built for sustainability (Wenger et al., 2002). As a result, educators can be equipped with problem solving skills, knowledge, and support networks that can be utilised to overcome potential challenges that may arise in the future.

Researcher reflections and future recommendations

As qualitative research is filtered and presented through the lens of the researchers, it is appropriate to conclude this chapter with some reflections and directions to consider for future educators and researchers. The co-authors of this chapter now reflect on the research experience.

Dr Chris Edwards' reflections (PhD researcher)

My reflections on the research experience are filtered by my combined perspective as both a PhD candidate throughout the process and writing this as an early career researcher. Firstly, it is important to state that prior to this research, my background was psychology, having completed my honours thesis while working throughout my studies as a disability support worker. Over these years, I gained knowledge, skills, and understanding as to how to best support a diverse range of learners across a variety of contexts, including special schools. However, my experience and perspective greatly differed from the school staff that we collaborated with within these mainstream rural and remote schools.

As I was born in Brisbane and lived in this city my entire life, it was quite eye-opening taking in the context during the long drives to these rural and remote Australian schools. Even more so, I don't think reading about rural and remote education can truly prepare a PhD candidate or researcher for the experiences within these regions. It was only after meeting and talking with the school staff face-to-face that I could truly begin to understand the complex and challenging situation that they were experiencing. This directly aligns with the emerging educational research, further highlighting how significant face-to-face time is to understand the contextual environment within an educational teleconsultation-based approach. As a result of this experience, I have developed a deep level of respect for school staff that operate in rural and remote areas. Similarly, I recognise the significant role that educational researchers need to play in supporting school staff in rural and remote regions, in order to best equip them with the necessary skills and resources to promote and sustain inclusive education.

Associate Professor Beth Saggers' reflections (EYBSP Project leader and PhD supervisor)

The importance of context cannot be underestimated and goes well beyond the notion of context as a geographical location or place. Context is so much more and includes a wide range of factors in the environment. These include: the geographical location; the teacher's values, beliefs, and training; the culture of the school community and region; factors that influence the individuals within that school community at an individual, class, and school level; and the relationships within that community, to name a few. Many of the contextual features of an environment are hard to understand without face-to-face contact and involvement in the community. The importance of building relationships with communities by establishing working collaborative partnerships with key stakeholders through ongoing communication is key. Relationships and communication are critical to work in schools at every level. The TCC approach provides a novel, user-friendly, cost-effective opportunity to develop and sustain working partnerships and communication with schools in a range of different geographical locations whether they are local, urban, rural, or remote. The key to the success of this research was developing an approach that could be flexible and responsive not only to the needs of the learners involved but to the needs of the school community and the people in it. It was important to not be afraid to let the research evolve in each school in a way that could respond to the contextual needs. The approach involved working with key participants including families, learners, and school staff to identify the needs within the school community. It then employed a multidisciplinary team approach to help support staff to implement strategies that could help support these needs in proactive and inclusive ways. It also sustained ongoing support to the school community to help them build their confidence in implementing the support, but also to understand how the ideas could be adjusted or modified if needed. As a result, a TCC approach is a novel way of supporting inclusive practices in areas that would previously have had difficulty receiving ongoing cost-effective support in this manner. The other thing that made this project successful was the fact it employed user-friendly options both in support and communication that did not add additional burdens to school communities but were easily employed into current practices and were responsive to their needs and teaching styles. The mode the TCC approach took also considered participants' preferences to maximise uptake. In a world focused on inclusive education, inclusive strategies and practices need to support education staff and families as well as learners to create a truly inclusive culture that supports a sense of belonging for all.

Future recommendations for research

The TCC approach was implemented over one school year, and while this provided promising results and complemented emerging educational research, future researchers should consider projects that utilise longer implementation periods. There are complex factors that should be considered as learners transition from one grade to the next throughout their school years. These are factors that future researchers could explore in order to further understand how teleconsultation can support school staff and learners long term. As CoPs are designed for sustainability, future researchers exploring this social phenomenon should consider the following questions:

- Can your project support a CoP over multiple school years?
- Can you explore the long-term values that community members develop through either the implementation period or a follow-up data collection phase?
- At the conclusion of the implementation, does the CoP continue to evolve as expected, or do community members revert to old habits?

Educational research has extensively utilised CoPs to promote positive outcomes such as academic achievement across a diverse range of learners (ElShaer et al., 2016; Wilson et al., 2017). While the larger EYBSP research project explored learner outcomes in detail, it was not within the scope of the research discussed in this chapter. Therefore, it is difficult to interpret how the CoPs may have directly promoted learner outcomes. Given the innovative nature of this research, there exists a gap for future researchers to explore how similar teleconsultation-based approaches supporting inclusive education through CoPs can directly promote learner outcomes.

This innovative research combined a cost-effective delivery option (teleconsultation within health) with a well-supported outcome of professional learning (CoPs within education) to support educators who have consistently identified as requiring additional support (Hepburn et al., 2016; Saggers et al., 2018). As this research exists in an emerging area of educational research, there are endless avenues that can be taken in order to best equip educators in rural and remote regions to promote inclusive learning environments. Therefore, future researchers can extend these learnings and further enrich the literature by exploring similar innovative research designs across a range of factors such as geographic context, audience, and implementation timeframes.

Note

1 Pseudonyms have been used.

References

American Psychiatric Association. (2013). *Diagnostic and statistical manual of mental disorders* (5th ed.). Arlington, VA: American Psychiatric Publishing.

Barker, K., Mallow, J., Theeke, L., & Schwertfeger, R. (2016). A telehealth rural practice change for diabetes education and management. *The Journal for Nurse Practitioners*, 12(5), 225–229. doi:10.1016/j.nurpra.2016.01.015.

Bice-Urbach, B. J., & Kratochwill, T. R. (2016). Teleconsultation: The use of technology to improve evidence-based practices in rural communities. *Journal of School Psychology*, 56, 27–43. doi:10.1016/j.jsp.2016.02.001.

Brownlee, K., Graham, J. R., Doucette, E., Hotson, N., & Halverson, G. (2010). Have communication technologies influenced rural social work practice? *British Journal of Social Work*, 40(2), 622–637. doi:10.1093/bjsw/bcp010.

Brunsting, N. C., Sreckovic, M. A., & Lane, K. L. (2014). Special education teacher burnout: A synthesis of research from 1979 to 2013. *Education and Treatment of Children*, 37(4), 681–711.

Christ, T., & Wang, X. C. (2013). Exploring a community of practice model for professional development to address challenges to classroom practices in early childhood. *Journal of Early Childhood Teacher Education*, 34(4), 350–373. doi:10.1080/10901027.2013.845630.

Creswell, J. (2003). *Research design: Qualitative, quantitative, and mixed method approaches* (2nd ed.). Thousand Oaks, CA: Sage.

Cuddapah, J. L., & Clayton, C. D. (2011). Using Wenger's communities of practice to explore a new teacher cohort. *Journal of Teacher Education*, 62(1), 62–75. doi:10.1177/0022487110377507.

Desimone, L. M. (2009). Improving impact studies of teachers' professional development: Toward better conceptualizations and measures. *Educational Researcher*, 38(3), 181–199. doi:10.3102/0013189x08331140.

Edwards, C. J. (2019). *Implementing a tele-classroom consultation approach in rural and remote settings to support a community of practice for teachers supporting young children on the autism spectrum and with complex needs in mainstream settings* [PhD thesis]. Queensland University of Technology, Brisbane, Australia.

ElShaer, A., Calabrese, G., Casanova, D., & Huet, I. (2016). Building a community of practice for engaging pharmacy students to learn in a collaborative research environment. *Currents in Pharmacy Teaching and Learning*, 8(5), 698–707. doi:10.1016/j.cptl.2016.05.001.

Frieder, J., Peterson, S., Woodward, J., Crane, J., & Garner, M. (2009). Teleconsultation in school settings: Linking classroom teachers and behaviour analysts through web-based technology. *Behavior Analysis in Practice*, 2(2), 32–39.

Gibson, W., & Brown, A. (2009). *Working with qualitative data*. Los Angeles, CA: Sage.

Glover, T. A., Nugent, G. C., Chumney, F. L., Ihlo, T., Shapiro, E. S., Guard, K., … Bovaird, J. (2016). Investigating rural teachers' professional development, instructional knowledge, and classroom practice. *Journal of Research in Rural Education*, 31(3), 640–641.

Guskey, T. R. (2002). Professional development and teacher change. *Teachers and Teaching: Theory and Practice*, 8(3), 381–391. doi:10.1080/135406002100000512.

Halsey, J. (2018). *Independent review into regional, rural and remote education*. Adelaide: Flinders University.

Hepburn, S. L., Blakeley-Smith, A., Wolff, B., & Reaven, J. A. (2016). Telehealth delivery of cognitive-behavioral intervention to youth with autism spectrum disorder and anxiety: A pilot study. *Autism*, 20(2), 207–218. doi:10.1177/1362361315575164.

Kline, J., & Walker-Gibbs, B. (2015). Graduate teacher preparation for rural schools in Victoria and Queensland. *Australian Journal of Teacher Education*, 40(3), 68–88. doi:10.14221/ajte.2014v40n3.5.

Laluvein, J. (2010). Parents, teachers and the 'community of practice'. *The Qualitative Report*, 15(1), 176–196.

Lave, J., & Wenger, E. (1991). *Situated learning: Legitimate peripheral participation*. Cambridge, UK: Cambridge University Press.

Lindgren, S., Wacker, D., Suess, A., Schieltz, K., Pelzel, K., Kopelman, T., … Waldron, D. (2016). Telehealth and autism: Treating challenging behavior at lower cost. *Pediatrics*, 137(2), 167–175. doi:10.1542/peds.2015-2851O.

Maher, D., & Prescott, A. (2017). Professional development for rural and remote teachers using video conferencing. *Asia-Pacific Journal of Teacher Education*, 45(5), 520–538. doi:10.1080/1359866X.2017.1296930.

Opfer, V. D., & Pedder, D. (2010). Benefits, status and effectiveness of continuous professional development for teachers in England. *The Curriculum Journal*, 21(4), 413–431. doi:10.1080/09585176.2010.529651.

Saggers, B., Klug, D., Harper-Hill, K., Ashburner, J., Costley, D., Clark, T., … Carrington, S. (2018). *Australian autism educational needs analysis: What are the needs of schools, parents and students on the autism spectrum?* Brisbane: Cooperative Research Centre for Living with Autism (Autism CRC).

Saggers, B., Tones, M., Dunne, J., & Aberdein, R. (2019). Tele-classroom consultation: Promoting an inclusive approach to supporting the needs of educators, families and early years learners on the autism spectrum in rural and remote areas in contextually responsive ways. *International Journal of Inclusive Education*. doi:10.1080/13603116.2019.1609103.

Trust, T., & Horrocks, B. (2017). 'I never feel alone in my classroom': Teacher professional growth within a blended community of practice. *Professional Development in Education*, 43(4), 645–665. doi:10.1080/19415257.2016.1233507.

Vescio, V., Ross, D., & Adams, A. (2008). A review of research on the impact of professional learning communities on teaching practice and student learning. *Teaching and Teacher Education*, 24(1), 80–91. doi:10.1016/j.tate.2007.01.004.

Walton, E., Carrington, S., Saggers, B., Edwards, C., & Kimani, W. (2019). What matters in learning communities for inclusive education: A cross case analysis. *Professional Development in Education*. doi:10.1080/19415257.2019.1689525.

Wenger, E., McDermott, R., & Snyder, W. (2002). *Cultivating communities of practice: A guide to managing knowledge.* Boston, MA: Harvard Business School Press.

Wilson, A. M., Delbridge, R., & Palermo, C. (2017). Supporting dietitians to work in Aboriginal health: Qualitative evaluation of a community of practice mentoring circle. *Nutrition & Dietetics*, 74(5), 488–494. doi:10.1111/1747-0080.12309.

Yin, R. (2003). *Case study research: Design and methods* (3rd ed.). Thousand Oaks, CA: Sage.

Zournazis, H. E., & Marlow, A. H. (2015). The use of video conferencing to develop a community of practice for preceptors located in rural and non traditional placement settings: An evaluation study. *Nurse Education in Practice*, 15(2), 119–125. doi:10.1016/j.nepr.2014.11.004.

PART 4
Conclusion

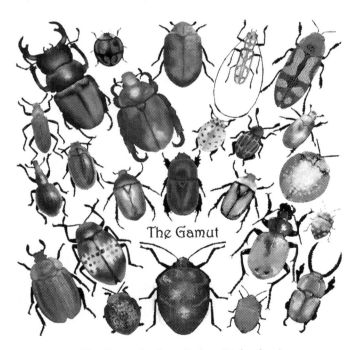

The Gamut (by Amy Forbes-Richardson)

'Gamut: The complete scope of something. Digital painting of beetles arranged in a spectrum of colours, inspired by the Yellow Ladybugs. I could have participated when I was young. I want to encourage acceptance of all people on the spectrum no matter where on the spectrum they find themselves. I have met some in the community who want to separate themselves from those they see as "lower functioning". I disagree with this.'

8

SUMMARY AND PROPOSITIONS

Keely Harper-Hill, Suzanne Carrington, Beth Saggers and Michael Whelan

> In this concluding chapter, the authors gather together the central themes presented throughout the book. In the face of an honest and sometimes sobering narrative for researchers, the key messages reinforce the importance that respect for individuals on the spectrum, their families, educators, and school communities is clearly actioned. Educational research communities are strongly urged to listen to the voice of individuals on the spectrum who justifiably champion that there be 'nothing about us without us'. This chapter presents a series of five propositions that capture the essence of the book, beginning with an appeal for inclusive education to take prime position at the top of the research agenda. It is apparent, however, that there is much work to come before research practices truly encompass the values of inclusion. The propositions for early and sustained engagement with individuals who are expected to benefit from, or mobilise, research findings provide a way forward for future research.

Nothing about us without us.

Since the inception of the Autism CRC, the research projects in the School Years Program illustrate the beginning of renewed thinking by researchers. The recently released Autism CRC *Participatory and Inclusive Autism Research Practice Guides (Version 3)* (Autism CRC, 2020) provides us with an opportunity to reflect what has been achieved in terms of research participation while also anticipating what could be achieved in the future. The journey towards co-produced research into inclusive education for students on the spectrum, their peers, families, and educators has only just begun.

> ...it is imperative that researchers who aim to impact student school experiences and outcomes consider not only individual teaching practices but how these practices can be implemented in a way that is compatible with the many contextual demands inherent within learning environments.

In this concluding chapter, we have drawn on each of the chapters to inform a series of five propositions. These propositions capture the collective voice of our co-authors and distil their key messages. They also highlight the complexity involved in conducting inclusive research within inclusive school settings. Layer upon layer of opportunity for inclusion exists within educational research and it is imperative that researchers who aim to impact student school experiences and outcomes consider not only individual teaching practices but how these practices can be implemented in a way that is compatible with the many contextual demands inherent within learning environments.

1. **It is both educationally and socially important that inclusion is put at the top of the educational research agenda.**

It can sometimes seem that inclusive education is viewed as an approach that is 'nice to have'. This viewpoint could not be more misguided. The move to inclusive education has led to growing numbers of children and young persons with disabilities in general education over the last three decades in many countries around the world (European Agency for Special Needs and Inclusive Education, 2020). As outlined in Chapter 1, inclusive education is a human right (United Nations, 2006) and one which Australia is legally bound to provide. Beyond an entitlement, inclusive education is also socially, emotionally, and academically beneficial for *all* students. Critically, inclusive education positively impacts on attitudes to difference, and students in inclusive schools provide greater social support to their peers and establish wider social networks. It is clear then that inclusive educational systems and settings provide an invaluable opportunity for building the foundations of an inclusive society (Hehir et al., 2016).

Despite its recognised importance, inclusive school practices are patchy at best. In Chapter 3, Saggers and Carrington clearly identify that systemic inclusion of students on the autism spectrum is not yet achieved and that 'we are not there yet'. This is particularly of concern because estimates suggest that 73% of students are educated in a mainstream setting (AIHW, 2017). It is little wonder then that we, among other researchers, are calling for inclusive education to be placed at the top of the educational research agenda. To impact positive outcomes and enable success for all students, including students on the autism spectrum, research needs to address challenges to inclusive practices and investigate those contextual adjustments that meet the needs of students with diverse learning needs. Researchers in the Autism CRC School Years Program have made a strong contribution to inclusive education research and provided direction for future research. This direction has been informed by the voices of students on the spectrum and their families as well as

Summary and propositions 123

schools, teachers, and allied health professionals on the issues which they face within the school environment.

Underpinned by a social model of disability (Oliver, 1996), there is a need for research to identify inclusive practices which are successfully situated within the social and cultural context of the school, classroom, and school community environments. Effective and flexible practices can support teachers to respond to a range of needs within the inclusive classroom setting. Such practices can facilitate inclusion and diminish segregation and exclusion of students and their families. While individualised responses and a greater intensity of support will be required for some students, this is not the same as working individually with children in order that they can 'be fixed' to better fit the school environment. It is about maximising the students' strengths in order that they belong and can learn and socialise in supportive inclusive classroom environments. We advocate for research that investigates the implementation of effective universal teaching practices such as those advocated within a universal design for learning (UDL) approach (CAST, 2020) which enable teachers to meet the learning needs of all students, including those on the spectrum, but never at the expense of their sense of belonging as a member of their peer group.

It is without doubt that more individualised and intensive responses to the needs of students on the spectrum are required, akin to Level 2 and 3 responses within a multi-tiered system of support (Clark & Dockweiler, 2020), and again we encourage researchers to look at the way in which this is achieved without undermining, and ideally by promoting, the inclusion of students. We are calling for research activities to inform and support school communities to explore and respond to their own underlying values and beliefs related to difference and diversity.

Throughout this book and as explicitly stated in Chapter 3, the need to engage 'the voices of people on the ground at the coal face of inclusion' is identified as key to research endeavours in this space (p. 37). Identifying school practices which support students on the spectrum and their peers with complex needs is not the end point. Research must also address how this knowledge is mobilised in pre-service teacher training, through teacher and school leader professional learning opportunities and collaborative ways of working such as communities of practice. It cannot be successfully completed in isolation, nor can it be informed only by the research literature. While potentially challenging to researchers, the agenda must be set in partnership with students and adults on the autism spectrum, their families, and educators.

> ...we challenge educational researchers to not only position inclusive education at the top of the research agenda but to apply inclusive values to their own research practice.

We have no doubt that some researchers will find it challenging to share control of the research process in order to co-produce 'their' research. In response, we propose that, as we have called for teachers to examine possible but unrecognised ableist values of their own, researchers are also encouraged to do the same. As such, we challenge educational researchers to not only position inclusive education at the top of the research agenda but to apply inclusive values to their own research practice.

2. **Progressive educational research about teaching and learning of students on the autism spectrum in inclusive school settings cannot be conducted in isolation of the school community.**

Wenn B. Lawson's descriptions of how involvement in research had left autistic people feeling *devoid of humanity* is a message that cannot be ignored; that researchers could fall so wide of the mark is confronting. Authors throughout this book have captured and described how the membership of a research team, and the nature of the relationships between team members, is a critical consideration for researchers who are not autistic, have not experienced being excluded, and are not familiar with current challenges in schools. Researchers must move from relating to members of school communities only as participants rather than as co-producers. We suggest that the successful development of respectful research partnerships between researchers and individuals with lived experience can only stem from the interrogation of researcher values as specified in the first proposition. If researchers view autistic students, their families, teachers, and members of school communities only as sources of data, then it is unlikely that genuine and reciprocal research partnerships will be established.

It is indisputable that researchers contribute a wealth of experience to autism research in terms of understanding the broader research literature and knowledge of methodologies. This 'research context' is, however, one part of the research story and no doubt to the consternation of some, we contend that it is not the most valuable. Lived experience of autistic students, their families, practicing teachers, or members of the school community provide perspectives that can impact the relevance and authenticity of research.

The voices of students on the spectrum, their parents, teachers, and all education staff provide a breadth and depth that cannot be discovered otherwise. There is no one experience of being autistic or teaching autistic students or of having an autistic friend. Research in inclusive schools not only provides an opportunity for research partnerships where previous 'participants' have a genuine role in the research process but also has significant benefits to the research and its findings. Along with such aspirations is an acknowledgement that this requires researchers to not only interrogate their beliefs but, in response, reconfigure the way in which they work.

One of the challenges in building equal research relationships with any non-researcher is in clarifying expectations of all team members and successfully communicating about these, and these were clearly expressed in Chapter 2. The specific issues for autistic members of a research team include giving answers that they believe researchers want to hear and is a very real example of a barrier to true co-production. Researchers must not only be cognisant of the power differential but need to act to rebalance this. To move forward, relationships must be based on trust, where members of the team have a shared understanding of roles and the actions and decisions of team members reflect an equal and respectful partnership.

Within the school environment, roles between educators, families, and students can be particularly hierarchical. This inbuilt hierarchy adds further complexity and brings additional responsibility to researchers. It does, however, also provide researchers with an opportunity to model inclusive practice as they develop genuine and respectful partnerships and facilitate active participation from project members.

3. **Effective and respectful inclusive research practices will shape and inform project development from the point of conceptualisation.**

If research is done differently, what will optimise the impact on student participation, belonging, and learning outcomes? As researchers, we can choose to further shape our research purpose and questions through the eyes of end-users. The perspectives of students, educators, and school communities will be critical for long-term impact. Independently developing a school or class-based approach which has a robust theoretical underpinning but does not meet the needs of teachers in the classroom, or is rejected by students, is unlikely to gain traction in real classrooms.

Including teachers and students at the point of research project conceptualisation will increase both the relevance of research questions and the feasibility of proposed adjustments or approaches. Further, early and genuine engagement with end-users leads to an approach that may be viewed as potentially useful by, and of interest to, school sectors, classroom teachers, and families. Fostering greater interest can positively effect recruitment, particularly at a time when teachers and schools are under ever-increasing pressures.

Co-production – whether through consultation, co-design, co-leading, or led by a school, students, or school system in consultation with researchers – can present dilemmas for researchers. As described in Chapter 6, resolving such dilemmas requires that the motivation for the research is clearly defined at conceptualisation and can be revisited to help move towards resolution. Relationships bound in trust become critical as does communication, and researchers are fortunate to have insights from autistic researchers and co-producers on ways to maximise successful communication. Therein is an additional, and critically important, consideration for researchers wanting to provide a voice to autistic individuals who are non-verbal or have significant intellectual impairment. While the Autism CRC School Years Program has yet to establish co-productive research relationships with students and young people on the spectrum who also have cognitive impairment or are non-verbal, we hope in the future that this will become a research focus of its own.

> *Including teachers and students at the point of research project conceptualisation will increase both the relevance of research questions and the feasibility of proposed adjustments or approaches.*

4. **The adoption of inclusive research practices should not only challenge researchers' own beliefs about disability, but motivate researchers to develop robust methodologies in response.**

The discussions above speak to an ethical imperative for employing participatory research methods. These methods will look different between research projects and may include a range of methodologies including participation as advisors or as members of research teams involved in co-production. The purpose of the research, however, has to be to improve the lives of individuals on the spectrum, their families, and educators.

Educational research conducted in schools is very different from clinical research which is frequently directed by the most stringent of scientific approaches often using quantitative research methods. In the Autism CRC School Years Program, knowledge mobilisation and research impact were often uppermost in researchers' minds and design-based research and co-design methods were adopted. The long-recognised value of the opinions of individuals who are expected to use, or benefit from, research findings (e.g., Finney, 1991) led to the inclusion of social validity measures by some researchers. Researchers were also intent on investigating the means by which educators were able to sustain the use of evidence-based practices in inclusive classrooms and schools; for example, through the use of communities of practice.

The Autism CRC School Years Program research projects have been peer-reviewed by a number of expert researchers, including autistic researchers. Each project is scored and then is presented by the School Years Program Director to the Research and Development Committee. The Research and Development Committee is a group of representatives from each of the essential partners in the Autism CRC and members appointed by the Autism CRC Board. The Research and Development Committee provides a forum for consultation and provides guidance and recommendations to the Board in relation to research undertaken with the Autism CRC.

We believe it is important to acknowledge the research approaches taken by researchers of the Autism CRC School Years Program because, particularly from a funding and policy perspective, there is frequently a drive to use only those approaches, practices, and interventions which have been established to be *the* cause of a positive outcome. Establishing causality requires confirmatory research aggregated from many projects. While some of the Autism CRC Research Program projects have asked if a discrete approach or intervention can be effectively implemented in an inclusively compatible way, these have focused on approaches or programs which have prior evidence of efficacy when implemented with students on the autism spectrum, often under ideal conditions.

There are, however, many reasons that we believe the assumptions on which many statistical approaches, including the gold standard of Randomised Controlled Trials (RCTs), are predicated, simply do not apply to research in real schools and real classrooms. We will briefly present only two of these: fidelity and randomisation. In terms of an 'intervention' under investigation using an RCT, the fidelity with which the intervention is implemented is critical. Assumptions on fidelity within schools and classrooms are brave. Experienced educators will identify that, no matter how good the intention, the school day is fraught with ad hoc and unexpected events. Further, the literature identifies that the way in which teachers practice is not only based solely on technical expertise but also from a position of responsiveness to their context facilitated (or not) by the relationships that they have with each of their students (Cordingley, 2008). Of course, it is the random allocation of participants to receive or not to receive an approach or intervention that aims to balance the known and unknown, observed and unobserved variability within groups and participants (e.g., Hariton & Locascio, 2018). In our experience, recruiting real schools and real teachers can be a challenging task even when educators are in favour of research and recognise the value of a particular study. We posit that the number of sources of variability inherent within any one teacher–student dyad, single classroom, or school would require participant numbers which may exceed the capacity of teachers, students, classrooms, and schools to participate in research.

In actuality, these considerations distract from the fact that the methodologies undertaken in the Autism CRC School Years Program reflected the nature of the research questions asked. The questions asked by researchers from the Autism CRC School Years Program have been far broader than 'Does this work?' and, accordingly, so have the methods adopted (Greenberg & Newman, 1996). An overarching aim of the Autism CRC School Years Program has been to support teachers to understand 'What will work *for us*' (in our context and in the way which we will deliver it) (as per Cartwright, 2011).

Many projects have not been so concerned with 'does this particular approach work' but have been focused on the 'why' and the 'how' of successful practice. Researchers have sought to understand and identify mechanisms for developing the practice of teachers and schools in order to meet the needs of students on the autism spectrum. Accordingly, the adoption of participatory research methods has maximised the impact of research into inclusive teaching practices and optimised uptake by teachers and schools across Australia. The intention for research that has impact has been a primary driving force of the research undertaken in the Autism CRC School Years Program and impact is reliant upon successful knowledge mobilisation. It is therefore not surprising that knowledge mobilisation is central to the fifth and final proposition distilled from the chapters of this book.

5. **Successful knowledge mobilisation is demanding and requires a concerted effort in order to meet the needs of its intended end-users.**

Mobilising research knowledge to the benefit of students and school communities across Australia is a significant challenge. The final section of this book has explored some of the issues which go hand in hand with this challenge and the subsequent response of researchers from the Autism CRC School Years Program. One of the messages arising from this exploration is that successful knowledge mobilisation from educational research requires an understanding of how teacher professional learning occurs within the constraints of real classrooms.

> *...successful knowledge mobilisation from educational research requires an understanding of how teacher professional learning occurs within the constraints of real classrooms.*

Learning to implement new practices, or to modify existing ones, is not an inevitable translation of new knowledge. By and large, teacher professional learning that leads to changes in teaching practices is a social endeavour. Many teachers expressed a preference to learn alongside, and through interactions with, like-minded professionals engaged in high-quality professional learning processes. Where does the responsibility for this lie – with researchers or with educators? We would argue both, but in different capacities.

It is incumbent on researchers to engage with their audience early in the research process in order to facilitate knowledge mobilisation which is more than an application of adult learning theory at the conclusion of a research project. Similarly, brief recommendations are insufficient. Responsibility to genuinely engage with end-users during conceptualisation of a project and the adoption of appropriate methodologies can be firmly placed at the foot of researchers. Our experience points to a need for tangible resourcing from funding organisations and universities so that researchers can make considered learning design decisions and efficiently develop multimedia resources that meet the professional learning needs of teachers and schools within the demands of their context.

Clearly, researcher efforts to genuinely collaborate with teachers depends on the ability of educators to contribute their time and energy to the process. In part, this means presenting research that will be meaningful to educators in their settings. Conceptualising projects *with* teachers will assist in the development of projects that resonate with teachers, potentially leading to greater recruitment and ongoing engagement with these educators. There is, of course, a caveat. Research that is meaningful to teachers can only assist to secure engagement and participation *if teachers have capacity to engage and participate*. The experience of research teams from the Autism CRC School Years Program indicates that a presumption of teacher capacity is made at the peril of the research project. It would therefore be naïve to suggest that research simply needs to be meaningful. It is our contention that it must *in the very least* be meaningful to gain traction with real teachers, in real educational settings.

Research that intends to actively inform and shape educational practice, rather than passively disseminate findings, has significant implications for research team membership, research methodologies, and, critically, research funding. Engagement with end-users through the research process is important and, as mooted above, dependent on many factors, not least teacher capacity. As described in Chapter 6, maintaining a balance between genuinely listening to the needs of classroom teachers while maintaining research integrity can be complex and there is no assumption that the Autism CRC School Years Program has 'the' correct approach to knowledge mobilisation. It is hoped, however, that the collaborative and co-design approaches described in these chapters will contribute to ongoing discussions on educational research that is both impactful and respectful. Research that also intends, from its inception, to mobilise new knowledge to the benefit of all Australian students, including those on the autism spectrum, their families, teachers, and school communities.

References

Australian Institute of Health and Welfare (AIHW). (2017). *Autism in Australia.* Australian Government. Retrieved from https://www.aihw.gov.au/reports/disability/autism-in-australia/contents/autism.

Autism CRC. (2020). *Participatory and inclusive autism research practice guides (Version 3).* Brisbane: Cooperative Research Centre for Living with Autism (Autism CRC).

Cartwright, N. (2011). A philosopher's view of the long road from RCTs to effectiveness. *The Lancet,* 377(9775), 1400–1401. doi:10.1016/S0140-6736(11)60563-1.

CAST. (2020). *Universal design for learning.* Boston, MA: CAST. Retrieved from http://www.cast.org/.

Clark, A., & Dockweiler, K. (2020). *Multi-tiered systems of support in secondary schools: The definitive guide to effective implementation and quality control.* New York, NY: Routledge. doi:10.4324/9780429023712.

Cordingley, P. (2008) Research and evidence-informed practice: Focusing on practice and practitioners. *Cambridge Journal of Education,* 38(1), 37–52. doi:10.1080/03057640801889964.

European Agency for Special Needs and Inclusive Education. (2020). *European Agency statistics on inclusive education: 2018 dataset cross-country report.* (J. Ramberg, A. Lénárt, & A. Watkins, Eds.). Odense, Denmark: EASIE.

Finney, J. W. (1991). On further development on the concept of social validity. *Journal of Applied Behavior Analysis,* 24(2), 245–249. doi:10.1901/jaba.1991.24-245.

Greenberg, L. S., & Newman, F. L. (1996). An approach to psychotherapy change process research: Introduction to the special section. *Journal of Consulting and Clinical Psychology,* 64(3), 435–438.

Hariton, E., & Locascio, J. J. (2018). Randomised controlled trials – the gold standard for effectiveness research. *BJOG: An International Journal of Obstetrics & Gynaecology,* 125(13), 1716.

Hehir, T., Grindal, T., Freeman, B., Lamoreau, R., Borquaye, Y., & Burke, S. (2016). *A summary of the evidence on inclusive education.* São Paulo: Alana Institute.

Oliver, M. (1996). *Understanding disability: From theory to practice.* Basingstoke: Macmillan.

United Nations. (2006). *Convention on the rights of persons with disabilities.* New York, NY: United Nations.

INDEX

Page numbers in *Italics* refers figures; **bold** refers table

Article 12 of the UN *Convention on the Rights of the Child* 52
Attention Deficit with Hyperactivity Disorder (ADHD) 23, 58, 60
Australian Advisory Board on Autism Spectrum Disorders (AABASD) 40
Australian Autism Educational Needs Analysis (ASD–ENA) 10, 71, 104–105; aim of 37, 38; challenges 44; co-existing conditions 46; contextual factors 45; contextually fit 45; data analysis 41; development of Phase 1 surveys 40–41; educational principles 40; emotional and peer problems 43; *inclusionED* 38, 44; individualised support 46; key findings 43–44; mixed methods sequential explanatory design 38; multi-tiered system 46; new education policy 45; open-ended questions 41; participants and recruitment 39–40; Phase 2 interviews 41; policy enactment 45; positive behaviour support 47; profiling strategies 37; qualitative open-ended questions 38; quantitative Likert scale questions 38; researcher reflection on research 47–48; research-informed practices 37; school-based and participatory research 38; self-efficacy 47; sensory elements 46; social elements 42; stakeholders 36, 41; teacher confidence 47; transition planning strategies 44

Australian Institute of Health and Welfare (AIHW) survey 9
Autism CRC *see* Cooperative Research Centre for Living with Autism (Autism CRC)
Autism CRC School Years Program 38, 45, 91–93, 96, 97, 125–128
Autism Spectrum Australia (Aspect) Autism in Education Conference 80
autistic community engagement 19
autistic space/autism-friendly space 54
Autistic spectrum disorder (ASD) 55
autistic voices: Autism CRC *see* Autism CRC; co-production research 52, 63; hypersensitivity and autistic brain 56, *57*; hyposensitivity and autistic brain 56, *56*; *inclusionED* 56–59; inclusive educational settings 59; participatory research 51, 63; safe learning environment 51; support strategies and interventions 55; treatments and interventions 51; voice research 52, 63

Bartlett, Trudy 50–63
Birds of Differences xv, 33
body language 22
Brisbane Catholic Education (Springwood) Support Teacher Inclusive Education 80

Index

Callahan, K. 90
Campbell, C. 91
Carrington, Suzanne 3–13, 17–30, 35–48, 50–63, 121–128
Cherrington, S. 94
co-design/participatory design: challenges 72; design stage *74*, 74–79, *75*, 77, *79*; develop stage 79–81, *80*, *81*; fuzzy front-end 73; implement stage 81–82; socio-technical systems 73; virtual co-design process 73
Cogs Will Turn Just Differently xvi, 67
Coldwell, M. 90
Cologon, K. 6–8, 11, 12, 62
communities of practice (CoPs): challenges 102; elements *103*, 103–104; teleconsultation *see* tele-classroom consultation (TCC) approach
Community-based participatory research (CBPR) 51
Convention on the Rights of Persons with Disabilities (CRPD) 4
Cooper, A. 91
Cooperative Research Centre for Living with Autism (Autism CRC) 3, 19, 20; collaborative research 52; education research 59–62; *Future Leaders Program* 53–55; and *inclusionED* 60–61; inclusive research model 52; and leadership programs 53; *Participatory and Inclusive Autism Research Practice Guides (Version 3)* 53; research leaders 53
CoPs *see* communities of practice (CoPs)
custodians 97

data analysis: efficient discovery 78; film streaming services 78; learning community 78; prototype website 78, *79*, *80*; visual and textual analysis 77, *77*
deBettencourt, L.U. 89–91
de Bruin, K. 6
Depp, C. 91
Disability Discrimination Act 1992 11
Disability Standards for Education 2005 11
The Diverse Learners Hub 70

Early Years Behaviour Support Project (EYBSP) **107**; Community element 109; cross-case analysis 106–107; Domain element 108–109; ongoing assistance and support 106; post-implementation findings 108; Practice element 109–110; pre-implementation stages 108; schools 107–108; short-term values 110
Edelstein, H. 91
educational research: development 125; human right 122; knowledge mobilisation 127–128; mainstream setting 122–123; methodologies 125–127; school communities 124–125; school practices 123; UDL approach 123
Edwards, Chris 102–116
Eldar, E. 8
Emergence: Labeled Autistic 18
emotional journey 76
environmental supports 10
evidence-based practices (EBPs) 89–90
Evidence for Learning 96
evidence-informed practice 90–91, 93
EYBSP *see* Early Years Behaviour Support Project (EYBSP)

Future Leaders Program 58, 63

The Gamut xvi, 119
General Comment 4 4
Green, V. 94
Guskey, T.R. 111–112

Halsey, J. 113
Harper-Hill, Keely 69–85, 88–100, 93, 121–128
home–school communication 9

inclusionED 38, 44, 56–61, 63, 70, 73, 82–85, *84*, *85*, 88, 93–99; efficient discovery 77–78; learning community 73, 77–78, 83, 84, 99; strong foundation 77–78; supported implementation 78
inclusive classroom: Autism CRC School Years Program 92–93; implications 99–100; mobilisation 91–98; research context 89–91
inclusive education: attitudes towards inclusion 8; beneficial outcomes 8; challenges of 9–11; definition 4; educational outcomes 7; environmental supports 10; higher-quality teaching 7; internal factors 8; international declarations 4; karmic actions 6; knowledge and understanding of autism 9; knowledge translation 7; leadership and policy 11; multidisciplinary support 12; policies and strategic plans 6; policy

and planning in Australia 11; positive academic and social emotional outcomes 6; religious beliefs and attitudes 6; segregated and inclusive settings 7; *vs.* special education 4–6; teacher education 11–12; type of support 9

Kerr, Jeremy 69–85, 93
Knapp, T.A. 36
knowledge mobilisation: inclusive school settings 91–92; researcher needs 97–98; teachers' needs 93–97
knowledge translation process: co-design/ participatory design *see* co-design/ participatory design; *The Diverse Learners Hub* 70; elearning portal 69; evidence-based verses evidence-informed teaching practices 82, 83; *inclusionED* 70; *Living Portal* 70; national conversation with teachers 69; online peer networks 71–72; professional learning opportunities 71; recommendations 82; research translation toolkit 83; text to rich media reimagining 82

Lamont, A.E. 92
Lave, J. 103
Lawson, Wenn B. 17–30
Layers of Community v, xv
learning communities 76
Lebowitz, B.D. 91
Levin, B. 91
Lilley, R. 18
Living Portal 70
Luiselli, J.K. 90

Mann, G. 5
Marder, T. 89–90, 91
Markle, R.S. 92
Mavropoulou, S. 5
medical model of disability 5
Mentimeter 80
My Helping Hands xv, 1

National Autism Center (NAC) 90
National Professional Development Center on Autism Spectrum Disorders (NPDC) 90
nationwide needs analysis 37
Nelson, J. 91
Netflix 78
Nicolaidis, C. 51

one-size-fits-all strategy 59, 60, 62
online peer networks 71–72

The *Participatory and Inclusive Autism Research Practice Guides* 19, 20, 53
Pellicano, Liz/Pellicano, Elizabeth 19, 51
Powers, B.A. 36
Prizant, B.M. 17
problem-solving process 36
Professional Learning Community (PLC) 59

Queensland Athletes With Disabilities (AWD) Futsal Team Coach 59

Randomised Controlled Trials (RCTs) 126
Ravet, J. 36
Raymaker, D. 51
Read, R. 91
Reed, D.D. 90
Reed, P. 8
Reilly, D. 73
Removing Learner Barriers for Students on the Autism Spectrum 59
Research and Development Committee 126
research evidence 8, 9, 36, 37, 89, 91, 92, 96
research practice: ADHD 23; autistic community engagement 19; body language 22; clarity and expectations 23–25; coercing 19; co-production 27–28; *Emergence: Labeled Autistic* 18; equal participation and equal value 25; families 26–27; five-day Research Academy upskilling event 22; individual autistic cognitive style 23; levels of community participation 19; parent–teacher relationships 18; participatory and inclusive autism research practice guides 20; partnerships 28–29; planning and conducting 19; process of engagement 22; psychiatric and neurodevelopmental research 17; public awareness and acknowledgement 18; reflections 29–30; research co-production 19; research participants 21; sensory distraction 21–22; shared interest 26; 'Taking autistic testimony seriously' 18; termination 26; virtual gathering 25
rights- and needs-based perspective 36

Saggers, Beth 3–13, 35–48, 88–100, 102–116, 121–128
sensory distraction 21–22, 27, 29
Sharples, J. 90–91
short-term values 104, 108, 110, 112
social model of disability 5, 12, 45, 61, 62, 123
social validity 90
Sohn, J. 91
special education 4–6
special education program (SEP) 54, 58
strengths-based approach 62
Subba, A.B. 6
Sustainable Development Goals (SDGs) 4
Sylvia Rodger Academy 20

talk aloud protocol 82
TCC approach *see* tele-classroom consultation (TCC) approach
teacher judgement 71, 91, 93
tele-classroom consultation (TCC) approach: benefits 104–105; education policy 112–114; education practice 110–112; EYBSP research project 105–110, **107**; professional learning challenges 104; recommendations 115–116; researcher reflections 114–115
Transition Models of Practice 96

universal design for learning (UDL) approach 123
utilisation projects 98

visual mapping exercise 75, *75*

Waddington, E. 8
Wenger, E. 103, 109
Whelan, Michael 69–85, 88–100, 93, 121–128
whole-school approach 11

Zelenko, Oksana 69–85, 93